SEIZE FREEDOM!

Culture of Enterprise series

Previously published:

Human Goods, Economic Evils:
A Moral Approach to the Dismal Science
Edward Hadas

Third Ways:
How Bulgarian Greens, Swedish Housewives, and
Beer-Swilling Englishmen Created Family-Centered Economies—
and Why They Disappeared
Allan C. Carlson

A Path of Our Own:
An Andean Village and Tomorrow's Economy of Values
Adam K. Webb

Econoclasts:
The Rebels Who Sparked the Supply-Side Revolution
and Restored American Prosperity
Brian Domitrovic

Toward a Truly Free Market:
A Distributist Perspective on the Role of Government, Taxes, Health Care,
Deficits, and More
John C. Médaille

Redeeming Economics:
Rediscovering the Missing Element
John D. Mueller

SEIZE FREEDOM!

AMERICAN TRUTHS AND RENEWAL IN A CHAOTIC AGE

Thaddeus G. McCotter

ISI
BOOKS

Wilmington, Delaware

The Culture of Enterprise series is supported by a grant from the John Templeton Foundation. The Intercollegiate Studies Institute gratefully acknowledges this support.

McCotter, Thaddeus G.
    Seize freedom! / Thaddeus G. McCotter.
    p. cm.
    Includes bibliographical references and index.
    ISBN 978-1-935191-66-7

    1. United States—Politics and government—21st century.
    2. Right and left (Political science)—United States.
    3. Liberty. I. Title.

JK275M336 2010
320.973—dc22   2010035364

ISI Books
Intercollegiate Studies Institute
3901 Centerville Road
Wilmington, DE 19807-1938
www.isibooks.org

To Rita, George, Tim, and Emilia;
For Our Free Republic

Freedom and not servitude is the cure of anarchy; as religion, and not atheism, is the true remedy for superstition.

—Edmund Burke

TABLE OF
CONTENTIOUSNESS

FOREWORD: MARCH!   11
    by Greg Gutfeld

CHAPTER 1
    What We Face   17

CHAPTER 2
    "The Science of Idiocy"   29

CHAPTER 3
    Too Free to Fail   59

CHAPTER 4
    Win Our War for Freedom   93

CHAPTER 5
    Deter the Dragon   115

CHAPTER 6
    Cherish Life   139

CHAPTER 7
    Our Blessed Sanctuary of Liberty   165

APPENDIX
    Conservatism 101   173

ACKNOWLEDGMENTS
    I Thank, Therefore I Am   187

INDEX   191

Foreword: March!

Greg Gutfeld

It's not hard—or even very worthwhile—to try and find a politician who can "articulate." They're pretty much everywhere these days, thanks in part to Teleprompters, speech coaches, and after-work Toastmaster meetings.

However, it's not very often you can find a politician who can put two words together that not only really mean something but are actually funny. Congressman Thaddeus McCotter not only can put two words together that are actually funny—but sometimes I've seen him do it with three, four, even five words. In the world of politics, McCotter is unmatched in the arena of articulation. He not only completes sentences, he basically humiliates them in a back alley. It boggles the mind that this man works in Congress. What did he do to deserve such punishment?

I got to know the good congressman through his guest appearances on my show *Red Eye*, a program he really has no business being on, for I'm certain in his future lie golden opportunities that only an appearance on *Red Eye* can ruin in a heartbeat. Amazingly, however, "T-Mac" (as Dennis Miller branded him) has managed to do the show repeatedly without ever besmirching himself—probably because he focuses all of his energies on besmirching me.

It's true: there are few people left on this planet good at the old-fashioned insult, and T-Mac is one of them. He may look like your basic run-of-the-mill evil Republican cast by Beatty, Clooney, or Soderbergh in their latest pro-Commie manifesto, but what lurks beneath the McCotter skin is a Don Rickles screaming to get out. And when he gets out, it's actually a good thing. His insults aren't just meaningful, and truthful; they're funny.

But I guess if you could choose your tormenter, I would pick T-Mac simply because he's one of the few politicians I've met who's genuinely *smart*. Not smart in that smooth "I went to Harvard, took over dad's business, and married Buffy" kind of way, but "I'm so smart it should scare the hell out of you" smart. That's how smart T-Mac is. And once you start reading the book you have in your hands, you will realize you aren't reading the latest tome by some white-haired bureaucrat with a ghostwriter (note: T-Mac has no hair, first of all). There's very little room in here for warmed-over platitudes and soft-focus photos of your author playing with a puppy. (T-Mac doesn't own a puppy.) He doesn't write like a congressman; he writes like a writer—because he is a writer.

In my view, T-Mac makes the most unlikely politician, because the people need him more than he needs popularity. His permanent grin of bemusement suggests that he already knows this, but the fact is: being a congress-man seems a step down for a man who could write books on philosophy in between playing guitar solos behind his head at White House picnics. (He's done the latter.) In this one sense, he is the anti-Obama. I cannot imagine Obama being anything but a politician, much like the Clinton of your choice. But with T-Mac, I can imagine him being everything *but* a politician: a professor of philosophy, a monk, a CEO, a character actor, a paid professional killer whose chosen weapon is a guitar's G string, you name it—I'm guessing he'd be great at it. Especially the G string part.

T-Mac is an authentic, old-school conservative—meaning, he doesn't mind if you think he's the bad guy; he embraces it. Being a true conservative—which I define as putting the individual before the government, and having a kick-ass military—is what I like about T-Mac. And if you don't like it, I don't think it's going to bother him much. We need more conservatives like the congressman—the type who doesn't stay up nights wondering if Colin Powell likes him, or whether he might get a regular guest gig on Letterman.

In T-Mac's world, the concept of "the moderate" should be mocked, if only because it's a position encouraged by your enemy so that it might eliminate you and make their lives easier. It's simply another version of "if you can't beat them, join them," which might have worked for the French, but not for Americans. This makes T-Mac a throwback who will never forget two things: he works for his constituents, and Washington is nuts. (He's also never forgotten the chords to "God Save the Queen"—by the Sex Pistols.) Did I mention he can play guitar?

T-Mac is conservative, Reagan-style, and if you think that's just too scary for you, then lose this book and go read *Highlights*.

—*Greg Gutfeld*

SEIZE FREEDOM!

1

WHAT WE FACE

Our Epic Struggle

Right now, parents suffer sleepless nights worrying that they will lose their jobs, their homes, their health care, and their hopes for their children. In the War for Freedom against terrorism, families bury, mourn, and honor their loved ones lost in battle against our barbaric enemies. Reverent citizens struggle to make sense of an increasingly perverse society disdainful of—and destructive to—our traditional culture of faith, truth, virtue, and beauty, if the existence of these permanent things is even admitted. Parents sense American exceptionalism eroding, and fear they will not be allowed to pass on to their children the great nation they've inherited.

Amidst this turmoil, Americans have come to view the government as lacking their consent, and as a threat to their freedom. Ideologues and demagogues prey upon such chaos, just as the great conservative thinker Russell Kirk warned in *The American Cause*:

> What really creates discontent in the modern age, as in all ages, is confusion and uncertainty. People turn to radical doctrines not necessarily when they are poor, but when they are emotionally and intellectually distraught. When faith in their world is shaken; when old rulers and old forms of government disappear; when profound economic changes alter their modes of livelihood; when the expectation of private and public change becomes greater than the expectation of private and public continuity; when even the family seems imperiled; when people can no longer live as their ancestors lived before them, but wander bewildered in new ways—then the radical agitator, of one persuasion or another, has a fertile field to cultivate.

Demagogues, of course, are not a modern development. In the fourth century B.C., the Athenian civilization heeded demagogues who dismissed internal and external threats as imagined, insignificant, and distant. Prideful and pampered, the Athenians ridiculed the patriot Demosthenes, who pleaded with the people—"In God's name, I beg of you to think"—to grasp reality and preserve their liberty. The Athenians refused and reveled in false hope—until Macedonian arms crushed them.

Poised to repeat this tragedy in our own time, we are enthralled with ideologues' simplistic solutions and false comforts. Wholly or in part, we are ignoring, belittling, or denying our immense challenges, and the demagogues deluding us are rewarded. No longer do we honor the Latin charge—"Out of shadows and symbols into the truth!" Instead, we flit from the truth into shadows and symbols, where yawns the abyss. We have forgotten young Abraham Lincoln's antebellum warning of 1838: "If destruction be our lot, we must ourselves be its author and finisher. As a nation of freemen, we must live through all time, or die by suicide."

Our Four Great Challenges

We are engaged in an epic struggle to conserve our cherished way of life. But rather than despair, at this time we must recall that Americans have always overcome great challenges and inspired the world.

Through the pivotal middle decades of the twentieth century, America's Greatest Generation overcame four great challenges:

◆ The social, economic, and political upheavals of industrialization
◆ A world war against evil enemies
◆ The Soviet Union as a strategic threat and rival model of governance
◆ The moral struggle of the civil rights movement

Now, our Global Generation must overcome four great challenges:

◆ The social, economic, and political upheavals of globalization

- A world war against evil enemies
- Communist China as a strategic threat and rival model of governance
- Moral relativism's erosion of our self-evident truths

Despite the parallels, a difference exists: the Greatest Generation faced their great challenges *consecutively*; our Global Generation faces our great challenges *simultaneously*.

Our great challenges manifest themselves in a global recession and War for Freedom against terrorism. In response, a leftist administration and its radical Congress have taken America in a "new direction"—backward to the 1970s. The Left has proven too costly, too crazy, too quickly, giving Americans:

- More deficits and debt
- More spending and taxes
- More unemployment
- More government
- Less freedom

Ideologically blinded, the Left has responded to our great challenges by making big government larger and more expensive, leaving sovereign Americans less powerful and more indebted. The Left wants big government to bury our freedom.

Instead, our freedom will bury big government.

We the People are at our best when challenged. It is up to us, America's sovereign citizens, to prevent ideologues and demagogues from reaping a bitter harvest in the "fertile field" of uncertainty and discontent. It is up to us to reassert America's enduring truths. It is up to us to determine freedom's future in these transformational times.

America Is a Country

The first step to transcending these great challenges is to rid ourselves of ideology. As was his wont, Ronald Reagan hit the nail on the head:

> Conservatism is the antithesis of the kind of ideological fanaticism that has brought so much horror and destruction to the world. The common sense and common decency of ordinary men and women, working out their own lives in their own way—this is the heart of American conservatism today. Conservative wisdom and principles are derived from a willingness to learn—not just from what is going on now, but from what has happened before.

Ideologues fit the world to their minds; conservatives fit their minds to the world. Ideologues believe politics encompasses life; conservatives believe politics is only a part of life. Ideologues believe they possess an abstract, absolute truth that can compel an imperfect humanity to attain a terrestrial paradise; conservatives believe in self-evident truths and the traditional rights and duties found in an imperfect humanity's wisdom, customs, and community institutions that have developed over the generations. As a result, ideology is an act of negation and hate; conservatism is an act of creation and love.

Little wonder that a plurality of Americans say they are "conservative," though this is more a philosophical position than political. Most people dislike radical change and crazy schemes. They know America isn't a bureaucracy or an economy, America is a country. Living real life's sorrows and joys, Americans want elected servants with the hearts to treat people as souls, not statistics, and to empathize with their trials and dreams. They demand honest, realistic answers to stem the rising tide of chaos in this ideologically riven time and to restore order, justice, and freedom to our American home.

It is incumbent upon us to reassert the centrality of the human soul in making public policy; return power and opportunity from governmental and bureaucratic institutions to American citizens; defend our blessed sanctuary of liberty in a lethal world; perpetuate American exceptionalism for our children; and never allow ideology to blind us to this reality.

Our Enduring Duty

Our enduring duty, then, is clear. We must:

- ◆ Expand liberty and self-government
- ◆ Conserve our cherished way of life and its foundations of faith, family, community, and country
- ◆ Empower Americans to achieve constructive, necessary change by limiting government
- ◆ Defend America's national security

The American Revolution's experiment in liberty and self-government lit a fire of freedom around the world, carried forward and nurtured for generations. Americans cannot allow that fire to be dimmed.

Unfortunately, the Left has been putting out that fire. Its attempts to swell government have reduced sovereign Americans from the masters of their destiny to the serfs of governmental dependency. The Left is not "progressive." The Left is "regressive," because it invariably increases big government at the expense of self-government. Thankfully, We the People know that true progress is the expansion of freedom. We know, too, that if America falters or fails in her "last full measure of devotion" to freedom, there is no other nation to replace her. After all, if we turn our backs on freedom, who will take our place and carry its torch?

Equally, we must not cede to big government our sovereign power to devise individual and collective solutions to our problems in the pursuit of our happiness. Tyrants claim that absolute order must precede their people's paltry snippets of liberty . . . which never come. But we understand freedom's paradox: personal liberty leads to national prosperity and security by *freeing* Americans to establish the true roots of American order. This is accomplished through the voluntary and virtuous individual, familial, and communal associations that inspire and guide a free people to conquer challenges.

Further, we must limit government to empower Americans to achieve constructive, necessary change. As Russell Kirk noted: "Permanence and change must be recognized and reconciled in a vigorous society. . . . Just how much change a society requires, and what sort of change, depend upon the circumstances of an age and a nation." In every age, big government doesn't stop chaos; big government *is* chaos. The federal government cannot keep inflating itself with higher taxes, spending, and regulations. Government must be reined in so that Americans can achieve the *constructive* change we need.

Finally, even if we promote liberty and self-government at home, we must defend America from her enemies abroad. A balanced budget alone will not preserve our freedom. In a bittersweet irony, it is our very existence as a free people that makes us the target of tyrants and terrorists around the globe. So long as we live as a free people, we inspire oppressed peoples to throw off the yoke of their subjugators—and their subjugators know this. We must be ever vigilant and strong to deter and defeat them.

Our Permanent Principles

In fulfilling our enduring duty, we must be guided by five permanent principles:

- ◆ Our liberty is from God, not the government
- ◆ Our sovereignty rests is in our souls, not the soil
- ◆ Our security is through strength, not surrender
- ◆ Our prosperity is from the private sector, not the public sector
- ◆ Our truths are self-evident, not relative

If our rights came from government, our rights can be taken by government. This theory of governance inverts the fundamental premise of the American Revolution: that government is established to protect our inalienable rights, which come from a higher source than government. Recognizing that our rights come from God, not man, protects our rights by asserting that government is subservient to the sovereign people.

Logically and rightly, the sovereignty of our nation is vested in the people, not an imaginary "Fatherland," bureaucracy, or crown. It lives in the hearts and minds of all Americans. This is the reason American government must be a limited government. If big government is allowed to dictate the rights of citizens, the people are no longer sovereign and America's revolutionary experiment in freedom and self-government is undone.

Historically, tyrants have viewed the democratic institutions of free nations as a sign of weakness. As Jean-François Revel observed in *How Democracies Perish*, totalitarian nations' initial advantages in mobilizing for and waging war tempt them to bully and blackmail democracies into appeasing them. Consequently, America's surest path to disabusing these rulers of such dangerous illusions is to practice the policy of "peace through strength" and prudently expand liberty to ensure our security.

Though we expect government to protect our national security, we should not seek "economic security" from the state. Dependence on government largesse precludes people's independent pursuit of happiness, degrades their dignity of self-reliance, and diminishes their prosperity, liberty, and sovereignty.

Crucially, a cancerous threat to our liberty, sovereignty, security, and prosperity is moral relativism. We are a nation built upon self-evident truths, not self-serving rationalizations. If moral relativism is allowed to erode these truths, we will lack a common moral compass, betray our national purpose, and devolve into heartless hedonists ripe for serfdom.

Blood, Sweat, Toil, and Love

This will not be the fate of our American civilization, for which generations of citizens have sacrificed their blood, sweat, toil, and love to make great.

Sure, some Americans consider themselves the cosmopolitan inhabitants of a new, global "post-American" order. They disdain their inheritance from the late "American Century." These callow, unwitting ideologues deem traditional American virtues, sacrifices, and strengths too steady to be trendy, too antiquated to be saved.

They are wrong.

Our freedom is too precious to be squandered upon or usurped by big government. Thankfully, the majority of Americans know that the twenty-first century's Freedom Paradigm is this: Good government empowers citizens by expanding freedom and self-government.

Embracing this verity during our nation's foundational trial by fire, Abigail Adams proclaimed, "I know America capable of anything she undertakes with spirit and vigor." To us, the heirs of America's revolutionary experiment in liberty and self-government, her faith rings true today, here on the cusp of our nation's newest birth of freedom.

Today, America's ultimate strength and salvation

remains her free people. We will not let her down. We will seize our freedom; lead today to shape tomorrow as an unparalleled age of liberty, prosperity, and peace; and honor our sacred duty to bequeath our exceptional nation to future generations of free Americans.

2

"THE SCIENCE OF IDIOCY"

An Intellectually Transmitted Disease

Normal people spend a lot time wondering why things have gotten so nuts. The reason is ideology. This is no new revelation. At its advent, John Adams deemed ideology "the science of idiocy."

The first school of ideology was founded by Destutt de Tracy shortly after the French Revolution. The timing was no coincidence. Ideology sparked France's gruesome revolution, which, in turn, led the great British statesman Edmund Burke to excoriate ideology as an "armed doctrine." So ideology remains, for the French revolutionaries' intellectual descendants still subscribe to the philosopher Jean-Jacques Rousseau's rejection of religion, metaphysics, and traditional culture—i.e., real life—and his claim that the "science of ideas" would turn Earth into Eden. T. S. Eliot captured the hubris of such "educated idiots" when he observed that ideologues "constantly try to escape from the darkness within by dreaming of systems so perfect that no one will need to be good." Deluded that they were freed from this need, ideologues of every ilk have ravaged the planet in pursuit of paradise.

Russell Kirk diagnosed these fanatics' disorder:

> In every age there is much human discontent, and in nearly every age there arises some revolutionary movement which takes advantage of that discontent. A revolutionary movement . . . is not a truly reasoned social philosophy, but instead is what is properly called an ideology: a fanatic political creed that promises to its disciples what no simple political or economic alteration really can accomplish.

Ideology is an intellectually transmitted disease, one highly contagious because it claims to uniquely enlighten and empower. Those most susceptible to ideology are self-anointed elites who think they are superior to others; the downtrodden who seek to improve their oppressive circumstances; and ordinary people who fear losing their cherished way of life.

Presently, we suffer the real consequences of these ideologues' insanities. To restore order and sanity requires exploring ideology's origins, examining its effects upon both contemporary American political parties, and disabusing ourselves of its influence.

The American Revolution vs. the French Revolution

A reporter once asked Chou En-lai whether the French Revolution was beneficial for humanity. The Chinese Communist slyly replied, "It's too early to tell." Chou recognized that our world remains locked in a struggle between the philosophy of the American Revolution and the ideology of the French Revolution. The American Revolution was a restoration of colonists' traditional rights as Englishmen against an obstinate and arbitrary British government. By contrast, the French Revolution murderously subordinated individuals to an abstract vision of a collectivist state.

In the late eighteenth century, Irishman Edmund Burke advanced the conservative philosophy inspiring the American Revolution, while Frenchman Jean-Jacques Rousseau concocted the radical ideology spurring the French Revolution. Even now, our nation is divided over the validity and import of these very different revolutions, and this division exacerbates our tribulations.

Rousseau was like an engineer trying to build a car by making up his own laws of physics. A people and their society were just a mass of raw materials to willfully mold into Rousseau and his acolytes' illusions of perfection. Convinced that they were creating Utopia, the ideologues rationalized away any and all coercion and violence in their victims' best interests.

Burke, by contrast, was like a dutiful gardener nourishing a rose so it would flourish, not perish. The rose could

not be made from scratch or radically altered into an aza-
lea; its bloom was a divine, organic cycle of growth and
life which could not be changed, only crushed. Therefore,
a virtuous people must dutifully nurture their divinely
inspired, organically developed, and generationally inherited civilization and defend freedom's flowering against
ideology's grim reapers.

True, the men were not utterly dissimilar. Rousseau
and Burke both believed that societies could not survive
without change.

Rousseau's idea of change was a radical one: a willful
demigod known as the Legislator would find a suitable,
unsuspecting people; destroy the foundations of their lives
and civilization; and remake it in the image of a subjective, unattainable ideology that incorporated and excused
all excesses and immoralities committed in pursuit of its
proffered paradise. Once attained, this Utopia's perfection
would preclude any further need for change. Aping his
dream society, Rousseau stagnated. Finding his "truth" in
his own ideology, Rousseau lost his intellectual curiosity;
he became obsessed with implementing his unrealizable
vision; his vital powers declined; and he died in a semi-
catatonic state.

Experienced in the practical affairs of government,
Burke agreed that "a state without the means of some
change is without the means of its conservation." But to
be constructive, change could not be conjured from whole
cloth. While acknowledging that one "can never plan the
future by the past," he equally cautioned that a "people will
not look forward to posterity, who never look backward
to their ancestors." Civilization required the constant,

devoted, beneficent change effectuated by reflection and renewal, not radicalism and revolution.

This philosophical conviction led the elected politician Burke to fear the power of the state, while the intellectual Rousseau embraced and expanded it. "The greater the power the more dangerous the abuse," Burke cautioned. During the parliamentary debates regarding unrest in the American colonies, he concluded that "the use of force alone is but temporary. It may subdue for the moment; but it does not remove the necessity of subduing again: and a nation is not governed, which is perpetually to be conquered."

Ultimately, Burke averred that people must be ever vigilant and active in limiting the power of government: "[There is] nothing sublime which is not some modification of power." The state was subservient, receiving only certain delegated powers from the people. The power of the people came from the eternal, infallible font of civilization: God, who provided the "stupendous wisdom molding together the great mysterious incorporation of the human race" and the "action and counteraction which, in the natural and in the political world, from the reciprocal struggle of discordant powers draws out the harmony of the universe."

Humbly aware that humanity could not claim to know the unfathomable mind of God—let alone claim to be a god—Burke rejected the rigid deceits of ideology. Echoing Demosthenes before him, Burke begged free people to think: "The important thing is not to stop questioning. Curiosity has its own reason for existing. One cannot help but be in awe when he contemplates the mysteries of eternity, of life, of the marvelous structure of reality."

Rightly, then, Burke is considered the font of modern conservatism, because he understood that life as lived is beautiful—unless and until Rousseau's ideological spawn succeeded. Burke decried the inevitable result of the ideologues' efforts: "The law is broken, nature is disobeyed, and the rebellious are outlawed, cast forth, and exiled from this world of reason, and order, and peace, and virtue, and fruitful penitence into the antagonist world of madness, discord, vice, confusion, and unavailing sorrow."

Toward such unavailing sorrow we seemingly career today. Sired by the radical ideology of Rousseau and the French Revolution, the Left is warring with conservatives' philosophy of Burke and the American Revolution. Inexcusably, amidst this struggle many influential conservatives have themselves become ideological. This collision of Left and Right ideologies endangers the vital center of American politics. In the absence of balance, chaos reigns, while worried Americans detect a whimsical sound echoing down the corridors of power: "what shadows we are, and what shadows we pursue."

In the continuing struggle between the American and French Revolutions, chaos and decline will *not* be our final answer on the matter to the Communist Chou or to the next generations of free Americans.

The Tenets of Conservatism

From their annunciation by Burke, conservatism's central tenets have been philosophical, not ideological. Indeed, conservatism is the *negation* of ideology.

First, conservatives believe that God created human beings with inalienable rights, and that each person equally possesses sanctity and dignity. This foundation both protects a person's rights *from* his fellow human beings and requires a person's duties *to* his fellow human beings. The adherents of the "God is dead" school of thought make humans' rights and duties dependent on how other people—i.e., ideologues—subjectively consider them. The horrors of such ideologies ravaged humanity throughout the twentieth century and threaten the twenty-first century. For, as Dostoevsky's Ivan says in *The Brothers Karamazov*, "Without God and immortal life? All things are lawful then."

Second, conservatives assert that government was instituted to defend citizens' inalienable rights and to facilitate citizens' pursuit of the good and of true happiness. Therefore, government exists because people have rights; people do not have rights because government exists. Ideologues, from Rousseau's French Revolution to Marx's worldwide revolution, have turned this on its head by subordinating the individual to government—supposedly for the person's own good, of course. So when you hear the call, "Workers of the world unite! You have nothing to lose but your chains!" it's just an invitation to a fitting for fancier shackles, compliments of the totalitarian state.

Third, conservatives understand that civilization is founded upon order, justice, and freedom. All three pillars must be present and balanced for American civilization to endure. Order without freedom is tyranny. Freedom without order is anarchy. And the often contradictory claims of order and freedom are reconciled by justice—those social and political decisions attempting to resolve the competing claims of order and freedom for the good of a people. Of course, conservatives also recognize that people are imperfect and possessed of free will, and thus the balance between order and freedom can never be perfectly or finally struck. Therefore, like the ancient Greeks, conservatives realize that the paramount priority is the order of the soul, whereby individuals attain *self*-government by employing virtue to balance their liberties with responsibilities.

Steeped in the wisdom that human beings cannot be perfected, conservatives do not view the world as they claim it must be or try to force the attainment of an illusory Utopia. Instead they proceed from an understanding of the world as it is. They understand that politics is the art of the possible—that, as Burke put it, "all government, indeed every human benefit and enjoyment, every virtue, and every prudent act, is founded on compromise and barter." This does not mean, however, that conservatives are crude pragmatists. They employ enduring principles, as established and revealed through tradition, prescriptive rights, and custom within communities to balance the claims of order and freedom with justice, and to constructively channel change to make the world as it could be at that certain time under extant circumstances. Succinctly, ideologues think, "If society isn't broken, fix it until it is," whereas conservatives think, "If society isn't broken, don't fix it. If it is broken, ask the people most affected how to fix it."

Finally, conservatives believe that human happiness is endangered by every political ideology, because each is based on an alleged superior insight into human nature that will achieve paradise in our time. Divorced from reality, every ideology inevitably demands an omnipotent, centralized government to forcefully perfect an "unenlightened" and unwilling population. It must be emphasized: if unchecked, all ideologies end in terror and tyranny. Even the seemingly docile New Left that heralded the "dawning of the Age of Aquarius" was not immune. The internationalized New Left's less stupefied soul mates included the Weathermen, the Red Brigade, and the Baader-Meinhof Gang, each of which eschewed "flower power" for less pacific weapons of social transformation "by any means necessary."

Ignoring the central tenets of commonsense conservatism, ideologues of every ilk hasten Eliot's dismayed prophecy in *Notes toward the Definition of Culture*: We are "destroying our ancient edifices to make ready the camp ground upon which the barbarian nomads of the future will encamp in their mechanized caravans"—be it a camouflaged panzer at the Maginot Line or a psychedelic VW "Love Bug" at Woodstock.

Screams from My Father

I witnessed a skirmish between the heirs of the American Revolution and the spawn of the French Revolution through the windows of a Ford station wagon and my late father's eyes.

He was born in 1931, a first-generation Irish Catholic American. When his mother died unexpectedly, his father realized he couldn't work and raise two sons and a daughter alone. My father and his older brother were sent to the nuns at the St. Francis Home for Boys; his sister was sent to live at the Sarah Fisher Home for Girls. He earned twelve varsity letters in high school and earned a football scholarship to the University of Detroit (he was later inducted into its Sports Hall of Fame). After a knee injury ended his chance for a pro football career, he became a high school teacher and coach, a union member, and a culturally conservative Truman Democrat. While he supported his party, he also declared his unrelenting belief that all politicians were "bullshit artists." (More proof your parents get smarter as you get older.) Before he died at fifty-three from a heart attack, he admitted to voting for a Republican presidential nominee twice—in 1972 and 1980. Unbeknownst to me at the time, I was there as he made his decision to pull the lever for Nixon.

One early spring evening in 1972, my father—a powerful man who resembled a hairy fire hydrant—literally tossed my brother and me into our family's beat-up old "woody" station wagon and headed west from our Detroit home to Ann Arbor, site of the University of Michigan. Despite our repeated pleas, he wouldn't tell us why we were going there, but, as we pulled onto Main Street, he did tell us to lock the doors and roll up the windows. Pressing our faces against the glass, my brother and I watched the grimy hippies loitering about the town with signs damning some guy named "Tricky Dick," praising another guy named "McGovern," and demanding the war's end. My brother and I had never seen hippies in person, and soon we were trying to guess which ones were girls. (Body hair was not a dispositive factor.)

My father was not so easily entertained. Grinding his upper denture against his bottom teeth (his gridiron glory was attained before face masks), he flicked an ash from his unfiltered Lucky Strike out of the cracked car window and barked: "Do ya see those spoiled rotten jackasses, sons? If I ever catch you walking around with your hair down to your asses and waving signs against America, I'll put my foot up your hind ends faster than you can shake a stick at 'em. This is the greatest nation on earth!"

Following his outburst, it proved a quiescent ride home.

In hindsight, it was the Rousseau-sired hippies' infiltration of the Democratic Party that compelled my father to vote for Nixon. On election night in 1972, I overheard him grouse to my mother, "My party left me."

It hasn't come back.

Peace, Land, and Baguette

The American Left is derided for being too European. The charge is true, because the Left's ideological roots are in the French Revolution and Rousseau.

The now middle-aged hippies who earlier drove my father to distraction—and from his party—have discarded the Democratic Party's hard hats for raspberry berets. Oh, there are still some traditional working-class Democrats who love God and country, guns and their union, but they are an endangered species. The party's power base is the old "New Left" all grown up—or at least older, anyway.

The old New Left remains intellectually adolescent enough to advocate that America import European atheistic humanism, moral relativism, wealth redistribution, unilateral disarmament, government-run health care, abortion on demand, gun bans, environmental extremism, and group rights, among other continental flavorings. In a nutshell, Rousseau's wilted flower children still dream of dragging humanity back through millennia of civilization into "idyllic savagery."

Well, we all have our dreams, don't we? But these leftist ideologues have no right to impose their nightmarish aims. Nonetheless, the Left is hammering radical change through our traditional institutions and upon unwilling Americans.

Anointing itself Rousseau's "Legislator," the Left seeks to forge a new society in accordance with its subjectively defined "general will." To create this "new America" in spite of Americans, the Left attacks decisions made by a majority vote as the benighted "will of all," and connives to impose its own enlightened "general will." When frustrated by the electorate, leftist elitists use the federal judiciary and bureaucracy—both unelected and unaccountable—to force collectivism and their radical "civil religion" upon Americans.

In pursuit of its new civil religion, the Left attacks and subverts American culture to

- ◆ eradicate faith from the public square—not a separation of church and state, but the subordination of church *to* state—as exemplified by the ACLU's battle to remove the Ten Commandments from schools and courtrooms.
- ◆ promote alternative, New Age religions and radical cultural movements that provide a service to the state, such as political correctness and radical environmentalism.

♦ suppress the Boy Scouts of America and other intermediating, voluntary institutions that encourage
individuals to think in terms of their "particular
wills" (traditional morality) instead of the "general
will" (the radical civil religion).

♦ emphasize multiculturalism's "group-think," because *these* associations balkanize larger groups,
break their members' bonds with the existing
order, and hasten individuals' acceptance of the
new, radical civil religion.

♦ spread the amoral doctrine of personal "self-
actualization"—including abortion on demand,
active euthanasia, and sexual "liberation"—which
alienates individuals from their traditional morality and immediate community, and spurs them to
accept an omnipotent state.

Those who resist this cultural assault and violate the
Left's civil religion of political correctness are "forced
to be free" through the modern equivalents of exile and
execution: unemployment and media lynchings.

Denying that the government is subservient to sovereign citizens, the Left presses its collectivist agenda primarily through the termination of individual property
rights and the practice of wealth redistribution. Rousseau's
denial of private property in favor of community property
is explicit in the Left's class-warfare propaganda to "tax the
rich" and "spread the wealth." The Left's war on citizens'
liberty, sovereignty, and prosperity is now most evident
in its trillion-dollar budgets and stimulus bill, its calls for
higher taxes, its "cap and tax" assault on American energy

production, and its compulsive pursuit of government-run health care, wherein people will be taxed for the "right" to have their very life and its quality depend on the state's discretion. There is no clearer example of the Left's turning the state into the sovereign and the people into its servants.

Finally, an often overlooked consequence of the New Left's decimation of American culture through a new civil religion and collectivism is a lax national defense. Rousseau believed the ideal state would be small, isolationist, and based upon abstract reason. This most certainly cannot be the case for the world's sole superpower, which is the eternal target of tyrants and terrorists bent on enrichment and territorial expansion. Ironically, like the New Left, these modern dictatorships are the intellectual descendants of Rousseau. As a result, the New Left has never met a dictatorship it couldn't excuse and coddle with diplomacy while danger mounted. It is exceedingly hard to denounce one's ideological cousins as evil, especially when one no longer believes that evil exists.

Though incomplete, the Left's drive for a civil religion and collectivism continues to invert the American Revolution's philosophy to advance the French Revolution's ideology. This is why our nation is careening down a dead-end street of post-Christian, European centralized socialism and international appeasement. Unawares, many Americans are going along for the ride. For instance, today's entrepreneurial, Internet-empowered youth loathe centralization and bureaucratization in their lives. Yet they voted almost two to one for Barack Obama, who, like Rousseau's Legislator, seeks to impose "womb to tomb" government control over their lives.

If the Left succeeds, America will devolve into just another humble supplicant for EU membership, and our lives will be wasted toiling beneath omnipotent government. But what is the condition of the conservative political party that is supposed to stop the Left?

The Damned Old Party

Haughty conservatives once claimed immunity to ideology. They ignored Russell Kirk's caution: "There exists some danger that conservatives themselves might slip into a narrow ideology or quasi-ideology—even though, as H. Stuart Hughes wrote some forty years ago, 'Conservatism is the negation of ideology.'"

One of Kirk's correspondents recognized the early signs that conservatives were succumbing to ideology: "The conservative 'movement' seems to have reared up a new generation of rigid ideologists. It distresses me to find them as numerous and in so many institutions. . . . They are bad for the country and our civilization. Theirs is a cold-blooded, brutal view of life."

Nearly twenty years later, in 2006, the American people rejected this "cold-blooded, brutal view of life." In twenty-four months the Republicans' "permanent majority" vanished. Caught in the rush of events, they were too ideological, indulgent, and indolent to prevent an electoral disaster.

It was a bathetic descent. In 1994 the GOP promised to be a permanent change from a corrupt, forty-year-old Democratic majority. By 2006 Democrats could promise to be a permanent change from a corrupt, twelve-year-old Republican majority. Armed only with earmarks, strangled by ideology, and steeped in special interests, the GOP was buried beneath a wave of Democratic elections.

Let's set aside the sorrier aspects of human nature for the moment and concentrate on the ideologies that decimated the Republican Party: "the end of history" and "creative destruction."

After America and the Free World won the Cold War, the GOP succumbed to Francis Fukuyama's "end of history" myth, which asserted that the ideology of "democratic capitalism" had universally triumphed over all others. On its face, Fukuyama's ideology merited conservatives' rebukes. Events, however, conspired to give it credence and further its acceptance. When Soviet Communism collapsed, the victorious Free World was emotionally spent from the ideological struggle. Domestic issues came to the fore—remember the "peace dividend"?—and this new ideological contagion spread. Absent the existential threat of the Soviets, unable to foresee the dangers looming on the horizon, and charmed by the deceptive calm before the foreign policy storms, conservatives bought into the fantasy that humanity had reached the end of history.

In hindsight (because how can one have foresight at the end of history?), Fukuyama's theory was avowedly ideological:

> This realm of consciousness in the long run necessarily . . . creates the material world in its own image. . . . Hence the real subtext underlying the apparent jumble of current events is the history of ideology. . . . [The

end of history's] theoretical truth is absolute and could not be improved upon. . . . In the universal homogenous state, all prior contradictions are resolved and all human needs are satisfied. There is no struggle or conflict over "large" issues, and consequently no need for generals or statesmen; what remains is primarily economic activity.

If history was over, then what was Reagan's party of American exceptionalism and a strong national defense to do? Fukuyama offered a drab, managerial chore:

The end of history will be a very sad time. The struggle for recognition, the willingness to risk one's life for a purely abstract goal, the worldwide ideological struggle that called forth daring, courage, imagination, and idealism, will be replaced by economic calculation, the endless solving of technical problems, environmental concerns, and the satisfaction of sophisticated consumer demands.

Buying into this ideology that claimed freedom would magically happen sooner or later, the Republican Party dimmed the lights of America's "shining city on a hill" and abdicated its historic role as the champion of American exceptionalism. Instead it became the middle managers of American monotony. The GOP did not bother to notice that, like all ideology, the "end of history" myth claimed to be a unique, inevitable revelation outside human control and replaced religion's heavenly reward with a terrestrial one that was ineluctable and perfect—a universal world of democratic capitalism. Of course, reality did not conform to this ideology.

In Fukuyama's forecasting of international relations, the result was "garbage in, garbage out." He did not foresee the impending rise of terrorism, Iranian imperialism, Castro and Chavez's expanding Latin American authoritarian socialism, or the alliance between Communist China and Putin's Russia to create and advance a new model of governance—despotic capitalism—in opposition to democratic capitalism.

Exhibit A of this ideology's detrimental impact on the GOP was the party's support for the permanent normalization of trade relations with a Beijing regime which still asserts that liberty is a threat to its people's state-controlled prosperity and security, and which uses predatory, mercantilist trade and espionage practices to gut America's economy and security. Exhibit B was the abstract, expensive, top-down reconstruction scheme to transform Iraq into a "model democracy." This reconstruction approach had more in common with Lyndon Johnson's failed Great Society and Rousseau's Legislator than with conservatives' understanding that a country and its government grow bottom up from a people's enduring cultural institutions of faith, family, and community.

As November 2006 neared with an electorate angry about American casualties in Iraq, a sputtering economy, and congressional corruption, it became clear that the GOP's belief in the end of history wasn't the party's only ideological problem.

Fukuyama's "end of history" failed because it was an ideology. Nevertheless, in a case of "it takes one to know one," Fukuyama detected other ideologues corrupting the GOP's conservatism. He condemned "the *Wall Street Journal* school of deterministic materialism that discounts the importance of ideology and culture and sees man as essentially a rational, profit-maximizing individual." What Fukuyama and the GOP didn't understand was how nicely deterministic materialism—or "creative destruction," as the elites termed it—dovetailed with the "end of history."

Within a decade of Fukuyama's unilateral declaration of victory over history, the ideologues of "creative destruction" were boasting of their success, as evidenced in one proponent's remarks to the Institute of Economic Affairs in London: "The task before us [is] tidying up. The great battle of the twentieth century was between totalitarianism and freedom. The great battle of the twenty-first century is between the forces of creative destruction and those of destructive preservation."

Here in all its unvarnished materialism is the end of history. This is the ideology that led "conservatives" to falsely think materialist panaceas—notably the chimera of "free trade"—would solve all problems between peoples. Enrapt by this deceit, the heralds of "creative destruction" (for everyone but themselves) placed a greater value on saving five dollars on an imported shirt from a sweatshop than on defending the inherent dignity of individuals; than on ensuring fair competition and jobs for American manufacturers and workers; than on securing the national security of the United States from predatory nations like Communist China; and, yes, than on preserving the moral foundations of American culture, which secures and sustains our free-market prosperity. Sadly, it was an ideology made quite attractive by the remuneration it provided, large amounts of which happened to fund political campaigns on both sides of the aisle. Disregarding Burke's counsel that "a disposition to preserve, and an ability to improve, taken together, would be my standard of a statesman," pseudo-conservative ideologues and their GOP political hand-maidens mimicked Mao in hailing destruction as creation and preservation as destruction, and degrading humanity from courageous souls into consumptive statistics.

Decidedly not conservative, "creative destruction" was not an entirely new ideology. Long ago, Kirk lamented that conservatives could succumb to the "mild ideology" of "democratic capitalism"—the belief that the United States' "way of life and institutions could be universally implanted around the world, regardless of another people's culture, traditions, and unique historical circumstances." "Creative destruction" is the "mild ideology" of "democratic capital-ism" on steroids.

And it seduced the GOP into neglecting its duty to expand freedom and self-government at home. Confus-ing chaos with freedom, the GOP failed to propose policies that would help anxious Americans constructively chan-nel the changes necessary to conserve their jobs, savings, and homes, let alone their cherished way of life during our economy's wrenching transition from an industrial econ-omy into a global economy. Instead, Republicans and oth-ers condescendingly opined, "Don't worry, something will take your job's place. Want an earmark to tide you over?"

Viewing its task as managing the inevitable triumph of democratic capitalism and lecturing Americans to just deal with it, the GOP became ideologically corrupted, and its contempt for the public is captured in the first book of Chronicles: "For we stand before you as aliens: we are only your guests, like all our fathers. Our life on earth is like a shadow that does not abide." The GOP saw people as materialists subservient to their more enlightened government and abandoned all pretense of principle, crudely exchanging material benefits for (it vainly hoped) votes. As a result, the party did not halt the general culture's collapse into moral relativism and materialism; rather, it had succumbed to and spread moral relativism and materialism.

Too late did the ideological GOP glimpse the higher authority that would end its "permanent majority"—the sovereign American people. Despite corruptly greasing palms to ensure its survival, the GOP was only greasing Psalms' prophesy: "Our life ebbs away under your wrath; our years end like a sigh."

The Elephant Catches a Wave

In the wake of the 2006 and 2008 Democrat "wave" elections, pundits and activists lamented, if not mourned, the death of the Grand Old Party. Having squandered its majorities in the Senate and House and its control of the White House, the battered, rudderless Republican Party was expected to drift away to sink during the Age of Obama's realignment of America into a leftist nation.

In fact, the Left's proclamation of a radical realignment proved deluded. When Americans realized that the Republican majority had governed too ideologically and ineffectively, they had provided Democrats the opportunity to govern. Immediately, though, the Left took a cannonball dive into a cesspool of radicalism and statism and never came up for air. Such arrogant and injurious governance rapidly disabused the public of the notion that the New Left Democrats in Washington were sane.

Americans are inherently practical people who want gradual, constructive change, not radical, destructive change. Thus, by November 2010, the Obama administration's popularity had plunged; the Senate Democrats' majority was hanging by a thread; and the party's House majority was gone.

The American people were not about to be cajoled or coerced into surrendering their liberty to the federal government. They reaffirmed that America is a center-right country. But this does not mean that the public again trusts Republicans. The 2010 conservative "wave" election was a victory for the American people, not the Republican Party. The question remains whether the GOP has learned from its past self-imposed wounds of venality and ideology.

Bipartisan Ideology

While it is easy to identify left-wing ideologues by their superior airs, economic collectivism, moral relativism, and terminal Europhilia, it is far harder to spot the "cosmopolitan conservatives" who are, in fact, ideologues. These Gucci-loafered globalists consider America an international shopping mall, not a sovereign nation-state. Economic Darwinists, they are advocates of "creative destruction" for everyone but themselves. Their pet causes are trade with

Communist nations and amnesty for illegal immigrants. Accordingly, their favorite epithet to hurl at opponents is "protectionist"—even when what one is protecting happens to be America's interests. Advocates of deterministic materialism when they can make a buck from it, they demand that working families' jobs be outsourced and their earnings and/or retirements be slashed. They deny the existence of self-avowed Communists. They speak in euphemisms, and declare the "end of history." In their ample leisure hours, these cosmopolitan conservatives prefer the febrile climes of the Potomac, and while they date everyone but Americans, they mate only within their class.

Where cosmopolitan conservatives and "New Democrats" mate is in the "New Market State." This bipartisan gaggle of ideologues considers America to be nothing more than an economy and a bureaucracy that they will manage. They pursue policies from a global perspective rather than from a national or individual perspective; they are the booster club for international, governmental, and corporate centralization.

This ideological oleo combining the "end of history" and "creative destruction" is served up by Philip Bobbitt in his weighty tome *The Shield of Achilles*. Bobbitt begins by asserting that martial conflict compels changes in the constitutional orders of nations. While not quite concluding that humanity has reached the end of history, he argues that since the end of the Cold War nation-states have been transforming into market-states (either mercantile, managerial, or entrepreneurial).

Per Bobbitt, ordinary citizens have little influence over which type of market-state a nation will become. This is a job for powerful global elites. Bobbitt claims that "leadership for this move is likelier to come from the leaders of multinational corporations (MNCs) and nongovernmental organizations (NGOs) than from leaders of the national security apparatus and the political establishment."

Where does Bobbitt think these unelected global elites derive their legitimacy to make these decisions for us? "For the nation-state, controlling territory by the consent of the governed assured legitimacy. In the new informational age that has brought about the market-state, institutions can exist and wield power in a non-territorial space." This is a recipe for being ruled by George Soros.

If these unelected elites choose Bobbitt's preferred entrepreneurial market-state model, the state will be global, centralized, and materialist. With materialism dictating the culture, people will no longer be sovereign citizens to be obeyed but simply consumers to be managed. National security and defense interests will be subsumed and redefined within an international strategic superstructure designed to attain and manage global stability. Though globalization's interconnectivity and interdependence increases the risk of systemic collapse, Bobbitt argues that the goal of stability can be achieved through *more* global interconnectivity and interdependence: "The market-state requires that we think in terms of *global relations* rather than international relations." Can you say "too big to fail"?

It's obvious why a system run by unaccountable global "experts" appeals to ideologues of every ilk. The abstract, deterministic, collectivist, elitist, and materialist nature of globalism most naturally suits the Left, and its veneer of economic libertarianism seduces the Right.

This elitist ideology helped produce the core economic and diplomatic policies of recent administrations, which have, with but few alterations, remained intact under President Obama. It was this bipartisan ideology that advocated the unjust Wall Street bailout and its "too big to fail" theory. It was this bipartisan ideology that approved the permanent normalization of trade relations with Communist China, which, because of our massive debt and mounting trade imbalance, has led the United States to defer the defense of our interests to the demands of Beijing and other unfriendly holders of our trillion-dollar IOUs. It was this bipartisan ideology that promoted "open borders" as a solution to the problem of illegal immigration. It was this bipartisan ideology combining the end of history and creative destruction—along with all other ideological strains—that have so disordered our age.

Is American civilization now so enthralled with ideology that we are doomed to degenerate into ambivalence, depravity, and decadence? Are we to become akin to the moral reprobates who espoused a universal ideology of atheistic, dialectical materialism and sought to destroy the creative free will of the human soul and the existence of free sovereign nation-states? In the twenty-first century, are Americans to become what we once battled and *defeated*?

"As Yet Thou Shalt Not Pass"

In his *First Letter on a Regicide Peace*, Edmund Burke observed that at the very moment when some [states] seemed plunged in unfathomable abysses of disgrace and disaster, they have suddenly emerged. They have begun a new course, and opened a new reckoning; and, even in the depths of their calamity, and on the very ruins of their country, have laid the foundations of a towering and durable greatness.

At this historical moment, our duty remains to creatively preserve our cherished way of life. Through God's grace it remains within our mortal power to reject ideology; to reaffirm and apply our inherited, self-evident truths to the challenges of our age; to conserve what must endure; and to make constructive changes to reinvigorate our American civilization.

Employing right reason and moral imagination, we will reaffirm that the American Revolution continues to expand freedom and self-government at home and inspire it abroad. We will be philosophical, ground our beliefs in reality, and accept, as Russell Kirk wrote, "that there exists a moral order to which humankind should conform." Practicing "prudential politics" to combat ideology's "politics of passionate unreason," we will uphold "the better features of American civilization, of the life we know and live," and advance "prudent, gradual change [as] the best means for preserving the permanent things." And we will remember that conservatives "do not believe that life is mostly an exercise in getting and spending."

Stubbornly, some ideologues will still proclaim that we live in a "post-American order." In a nation besieged by recession, war, and chaos, they argue that Americans will sacrifice freedom for the Left's chimeras of big government and international appeasement.

Admittedly, because of Republican failures during this daunting time, citizens did momentarily heed the Left's siren song of nebulous "hope and change." But now, wide awake to the Left's real intent, the public rejects the rebranded but still injurious policies that were passed off as new ideas. Americans know the "stimulus bill" was a trillion-dollar obscenity of big-government spending that sends the deficit and debt skyrocketing, "saves" the jobs of government bureaucrats, and spurs the return of stagflation. Americans realize that "climate change" is a pseudo-science scare tactic so government can impose its "cap and tax" scheme for controlling energy production, raising taxes, and dictating people's daily routines. Americans recoil at the government-run health law that drastically curbs their quality of care and control over their own medical decisions. Americans understand that "smart power" is but a Carteresque call for peace through weakness.

Americans must hearken back to the stalwart leaders who guided our country as it surmounted other trying times. Presidents Abraham Lincoln, Theodore Roosevelt, and Ronald Reagan all entered office in turbulent, ideologically charged times. All three presidents opposed ideology's simplistic solutions and excesses, stayed true to their principles, were viciously attacked for it, and successfully practiced politics as the art of the possible to preserve our free republic's "contract of eternal society" between the generations.

Lincoln secured both the Union and its new birth of freedom. Roosevelt established the framework for, and expedited the growth of, our industrial economy and social safety net, and commenced America's rise as a world power. Reagan led the rejuvenation of America's morale and economy, its Cold War victory over Communism, and its emergence as the world's sole superpower. Lincoln the founder, Roosevelt the builder, and Reagan the finisher—each met Alfred Lord Tennyson's summons to "live pure, speak true, right wrong," and led America as it transcended the generational challenges of the time.

Reinvigorated by the accomplishments of these presidents and their generations of Americans, we take heart despite our trying times. As they did before us, we will seize our opportunity to sacrifice and suffer so we can transcend our great challenges and conserve our beloved country. We heed Reagan's warning that "freedom is never more than one generation away from extinction." And we meet Reagan's heroic metric: "Let us be sure that those who come after will say of us . . . that in our time we did everything that could be done. We finished the race; we kept them free; we kept the faith."

Yes, we will finish the race and keep the faith. And undaunted and undeceived by ideology, we will answer Orestes Brownson's soulful call to serve:

> Ask not what your age wants, but what it needs; not what will be your reward, but what, without which, it cannot be saved; and that go and do; and find your reward in the consciousness of having done your duty, and above all in the reflection that you have been accounted to suffer somewhat for mankind.

Though we may be down, Americans are never out—indeed, no honorable people ever are. It remains as in Tennyson's *Idylls of the King*, wherein a disillusioned King Arthur awakens from a haunting dream of disaster and by his side finds Sir Bedivere, who urges: "O me, my King, let pass whatever will. . . . As yet thou shalt not pass. . . . Arise, go forth and conquer as of old."

America: As yet thou shalt not pass. Arise, go forth, and conquer as of old!

3

Too Free to Fail

On the Bubble

The financial crisis was destroying families' life savings.
How the situation was resolved would determine the people's immediate prosperity and their future relationship
with America's political and financial institutions. An outraged president excoriated the elite who wrought this harm
upon the people:

> You have used the funds of the bank to speculate. . . .
> When you won, you divided the profits amongst you,
> and when you lost, you charged it to the bank. You tell
> me that if I take the deposits from the bank and annul
> the charter, I shall ruin ten thousand families. That
> may be true, gentlemen, but that is your sin! Should
> I let you go on, you will ruin fifty thousand families,
> and that would be my sin!

In 1832 President Andrew Jackson terminated the Second Bank of the United States and its control of the American economy, and affirmed the sovereign people's primacy in our free republic. To those who claimed that renewing the flawed bank's charter was needed for prosperity, Jackson shot back: "There are no necessary evils in government."

In 2008, during the first financial panic of the "New Global Economy," lesser leaders capitulated to the special interests. Blind to Russell Kirk's warning that "a society that thinks only of alleged Efficiency, regardless of the consequences to human beings, works its own ruin," a panicked federal government claimed that there were necessary evils in government and bailed out the financial institutions that had caused the crisis.

By unjustly transferring hundreds of billions of dollars of taxpayer money to irresponsible financial entities, the government expanded its tentacles into the free market and subordinated America's sovereign citizens to a combine of big government and big business.

Oh, for a spell it appeared to work—until it became apparent that the taxpayers' $700 billion was being used for the banks' bonuses and recapitalization, not for credit on Main Street. Now we scramble in the ashes of a *Brave New World* economy premised on the discredited theory of "too big to fail," which falsely claimed that concentrated power in a few interdependent financial institutions would preserve prosperity and prevent an economic collapse.

Unabashed by the very collapse that they once claimed was impossible, these bailed-out financial institutions seek to permanently socialize their losses onto the backs of working families. Allegedly this is the surcharge Americans must pay for having a financial system. This is absurd. The only price working families pay for a financial system is these institutions' honest profits. Regardless, the practitioners of the "too big to fail" ideology angle to divorce themselves from the consequences of their avarice and persist in advocating a hyperconsumptive, perpetually expanding economy controlled by expert elites. In *A Humane Economy*, Wilhelm Röpke revealed this ideology's core fallacy: "The idea that saving is, at best, unnecessary and may be harmful." According to Röpke, "Saving and good husbandry are represented as enemies of economic progress."

In a hyperconsumptive economy that encourages easy credit and disdains saving and investment, inevitably "bubbles" inflate and burst. During the latest crisis, a contracting economy claimed the jobs of homeowners, many of whom then lost their ability to pay their mortgages and fell into foreclosure. The value of their properties fell, and thereby so did the value of financial institutions' mortgage-backed securities. Credit markets froze as overleveraged lenders, mortgage-backed-securities holders, and their insurers faced imminent collapse. The housing bubble burst—just as earlier a savings-and-loan bubble and a dot-com bubble had burst.

Upon this cycle of bursting bubbles the industrial-welfare state implodes. To save it, the Democratic administration and Congress began borrowing and spending more than a trillion of your dollars to create a "government bubble." Ironically, this unsustainable fiscal chicanery will only hasten the inevitable. Big government and the finan-

cial behemoths are not "too big" or "too important" to fail.
They are too big to succeed.

Only freedom is too important to fail.

On the Bubble: The Implosion of
the Industrial-Welfare State

In our Global Age, government should not get bigger as our
world gets smaller.

During the twentieth century's Industrial Era, new
technologies spurred highly centralized and bureaucra-
tized economic enterprises. Big government grew to mirror this vertical model.

In the early stages of industrialization, Americans felt
powerless in the face of the economic, social, and political forces radically altering their way of life. Writing years
later, Röpke examined how these forces of "mass society"
affected human beings:

> The disintegration of the social structure [generates]
> a profound upheaval in the outward conditions of
> each individual's life, thought, and work. Independ-
> ence is smothered; men are uprooted and taken out
> of the close-woven social texture in which they were
> secure; true communities are broken up in favor of
> more universal but impersonal collectivities in which
> the individual is no longer a person in his own right;
> the inward, spontaneous social fabric is loosened in
> favor of mechanical, soulless organization, with its
> outward compulsion; all individuality is reduced to

one plane of uniform normality; the area of individual action, decision, and responsibility shrinks in favor of collective planning and decision; the whole of life becomes uniform and standard mass life, ever more subject to party politics, "nationalization," and "socialization."

The industrial-welfare state arose to ameliorate the public's economic, social, and political anxieties, which threatened the stability of our free republic. It spent the twentieth century creating America's "social safety net" and dividing the responsibilities for it between centralized corporations and government. But it was Americans' ingenuity and industriousness, especially in industrial production, that paid for both corporations' and the government's shares of this social safety net. In our "post-industrial," consumption-based economy, the domestic production void has been filled with unsustainable borrowing. As a result, big government teeters toward its breaking point.

During our Global Age, an innovation revolution spurs increasingly democratized and consumer-driven economic enterprises. Big government must be reset to mirror this horizontal model.

As during industrialization, today's Americans are vexed by the potent economic, social, and political forces radically reshaping their lives. But now American corporations are busy decentralizing into "virtual corporations" that outsource jobs to other nations to obtain lower labor costs and evade domestic laws and regulations. Such "rootless capital" being sent around the world in a keystroke to "low-cost countries" has dearly cost Americans their live-lihoods, reduced their wages and employer-provided ben-efits, diminished their unions' memberships, raised doubts about our economy's continued vitality, and, in cases of extreme economic distress, destroyed marriages and families.

While the human cost of this tectonic economic shift mounts, ideologues are busy trying to exploit it. But nei-ther anarchy nor big government is the solution. Shunt-ing sovereign citizens beneath centralized corporatist or socialist states will destroy our free republic.

Again, Röpke: "Once the mania of uniformity and centralization spreads and once the centrists begin to lay down the law of the land, then we are in the presence of one of the most serious danger signals warning us of the impending loss of freedom, humanity, and the health of society."

The solution is our twenty-first century's Freedom Paradigm: *Good government empowers citizens by expand-ing freedom and self-government.* Our future cannot rest in the hands of more bureaucracy and big government. The industrial-welfare state cannot be resurrected by more bor-rowing, spending, taxes, and mandates. Thus, our choice is clear: a humane, innovation-empowered economy or the soulless Servile State.

The Rise of the Soulless Servile State

Writing in the early twentieth century, Hilaire Belloc observed that formerly sovereign citizens were becoming subjects of the "Servile State." Belloc and his friend G. K. Chesterton predicted that the Servile State would be neither capitalist nor socialist. It would be both: big government and big business colluding to manipulate free people. In *Third Ways*, Allan C. Carlson summarizes both men's concerns, saying that they believed "the welfare state, with its cradle-to-grave benefits such as health care and food stamps," would merge with "monopoly capital into a 'corporate state' or 'state capitalism.'"

Carlson then recounts what Chesterton considered the symptoms of England's decline into a "Business Government" state:

> English leaders for almost a century had committed their nation to "new and enormous experiments," including, in Chesterston's words: "To make their own nation an eternal debtor to a few rich men"; "To driving food out of their own country in the hope of buying it back again from the ends of the earth"; "To losing every type of moderate prosperity . . . till there was no independence without luxury and no labour without ugliness." . . . And all of this "hanging on a thread of alien trade which [grows] thinner and thinner."

Chesterton himself went on:

> Private things are already public in the worst sense of the word; that is, they are personal and dehumanized. Public things are already private in the worst sense of the word; that is, they are mysterious and secretive and largely corrupt. The new sort of Business Gov-

ernment will combine everything that is bad in all the plans for a better world. . . . There will be nothing but a loathsome thing called Social Service; which means slavery without loyalty.

Contemporaneously in America, President Theodore Roosevelt grasped the cultural erosion that could lead our nation down a similar path: "The things that will destroy America are prosperity at any price, peace at any price, safety first instead of duty first, the love of soft living, and the get rich quick theory of life."

His warning is apparently lost on many in our time of "too big to fail" and the entitlement culture that increasingly permeates our citizenry. Preying upon this to centralize power and wealth for its own sake, the Servile State tempts citizens to trade their personal liberty and property for promises of economic security, as Röpke forewarned: "It is the temptation of mechanical perfection and of uniformity at the expense of freedom." Enticed by such riches and undone by their own foibles, free-market institutions succumb to the Servile State's grasp.

Case in point: Maurice R. "Hank" Greenberg, chairman and chief executive of American International Group (AIG) from 1967 until 2005, admitted how the insurance giant succumbed to this temptation upon his departure: "How did AIG get to this point? Clearly, risk management controls disappeared or were weakened. In recent years, AIG grew for the sake of growth, without regard for profitability, and its financial products businesses spun out of control." And when they did, the Servile State was there to take over the company and socialize its losses.

Too bad for us all that Mr. Greenberg and AIG ignored Edmund Burke's advice: "If we command our wealth, we shall be rich and free. If our wealth commands us, we are poor indeed."

And daily we get poorer from the disastrous economic policies of the current leftist administration and the Congress, as all the while we are prodded like cattle toward the Servile State.

The Servile State's House on a Slippery Rock

Giving a secular bent to the Tenth Commandment, the British economist Lionel Robbins noted that "the free society is not to be built upon envy." Sadly, the Left is bent on trying.

Leftists demand that we fork over trillions of our hard-earned tax dollars to a former community organizer so he can radically change the most prosperous and equitable economy in human history—ours—into a government-directed one. This ideological scam is monumentally ignorant of Americans' accomplishments and devoid of rudimentary political and economic principles.

One passage proves the point. In decrying America's "troubled economic past," the president avers, "We cannot rebuild this economy on the same pile of sand. We must build our house upon a rock. We must lay a new foundation for growth and prosperity." (Evidently, the decline in housing prices has downgraded our "shining city on a hill" to a "house upon a rock.")

This leftist cant posits that the recent recession invalidated the historical success and the very foundation of America's free-market economy. Rejecting the principle that our prosperity comes from the private sector, not the public sector, the Left cavalierly dismisses the storied, envied achievements of our free-market economy, which was most decidedly not built upon sand. It was built upon the virtuous work of Americans.

Ideologically averse to this truth, the Left feels that our prosperity comes from the public sector, not the private sector; therefore, government must tax and spend people's wealth to fix all real and imagined inequities in American life.

The White House, for example, seeks to erect "five pillars" of a radically altered American economy. Tossing sops to private-sector entrepreneurship and the free market, the president and his supporters pronounce that each of these pillars is founded upon new "investments." Such terminology is Orwellian: government doesn't invest *its* money; government spends *your* money. And it spends taxpayers' money in areas where no one would ever choose to invest his own money.

Combined with a multitrillion-dollar tax-and-spending spree, the Left's agenda paves a hellish road to higher deficits, more debt and taxes, stagflation, and a state-planned economy.

This slide to the Servile State failed in the 1970s. It will fail disastrously today. The Left has replaced the housing bubble with a government bubble. This government bubble will burst sooner rather than later, with dire consequences for Americans' liberty, sovereignty, prosperity, and, yes, security.

Fortunately, a concerned public demands an end to the Left's spending orgy. These citizens want a sound recovery plan based upon fiscal integrity. Such a necessary recovery plan should enable Americans to forge a humane, innovation-empowered economy.

The Path to a Humane, Innovation-Empowered Economy

In his September 17, 1966, speech at Worthington, Minnesota, Senator Robert F. Kennedy tallied the human toll of "centrism" (the force behind the as-yet-unnamed ideology of "too big to fail"):

> Even as the drive toward bigness [and] concentration
> . . . has reached heights never before dreamt of in the
> past, we have come suddenly to realize how heavy a
> price we have paid: in overcrowding and pollution
> of the atmosphere, and impersonality; in growth of
> organizations, particularly government, so large and
> powerful that individual effort and importance seem
> lost; and in loss of the values of nature and commu-
> nity and local diversity that found their nurture in
> the smaller towns and rural areas of America. And,
> as we enter the last third of the twentieth century, we
> can see that the price has been too high. Bigness, loss
> of community, organizations and society grown far

past the human scale—these are the besetting sins
of the twentieth century, which threaten to paralyze
our very capacity to act, or our ability to preserve the
traditions and values of our past in a time of swirl-
ing, constant change.

Through the ensuing decades, this price of bigness has
escalated, even though the forces of globalization run
counter to it.

An increasingly interconnected world economy benefits from decentrism, not centrism. Contrary to the claims
of big government and big business, globalization does
not require more centralization and bureaucratization to
"manage" it. Globalization encourages entities to become
more entrepreneurial, accountable, transparent, and
democratic. The Internet and other communication innovations have decentralized power from massive bureaucratic entities to individuals in our now consumer-driven
economy.

This global expansion of opportunity broadens the base
for innovation and entrepreneurial growth, and through
decentralization it fosters a broader economic foundation,
the greater stability of which prevents "systemic risks." As
long as big government does not butt in, globalization can
lead to a marketplace "too free to fail."

RFK would have well understood how globalization
decentralizes "too big to fail" entities to a more humane
scale:

To recapture and reinforce the values of a more human
time and place . . . it is not more bigness that should

be our goal. . . . We must attempt, rather, to bring
people back to . . . the warmth of community, to the
worth of individual effort and responsibility . . . and
of individuals working together as a community, to
better their lives and their children's future. . . . If this
country is to move ahead . . . it will not be by making
everything bigger, not by piling all our people further
on top of one another in huge cities, not by reducing
the citizen to the role of passive consumer and recipi-
ent of the official vision, the official product.

No "passive consumers," Americans are God's children, sovereign citizens, and not merely the sum of our
possessions. We reject the "too big to fail" ideology's soulless materialism, the consequences of which Russell Kirk
posited: "If material aggrandizement is the chief object of
a people, there remains no moral check upon the means
employed to acquire wealth; violence and fraud become
common practices [and] we must find ourselves remark-
ably unprosperous—and wondrously miserable."

A humane, innovation-empowered economy requires
decentrism, which, according to Röpke, "requires us to
stand for variety and independence in every sphere." The
individual's "center is God, and this is why he refuses to
accept human centers instead."

So centered, we can stem the cultural decay that has
brought us to the brink of the Servile State; attain an
innovation-empowered economy; and create a more holis-
tic, soulful American civilization.

The Humane Economy's Shining City on a Hill

Our free people and free market have made America's economy the most prosperous and equitable in human history. To improve upon this unparalleled achievement, we seek an innovative economy that still rewards good ideas, sound decisions, and hard work. At a time when the federal budget is ballooning and family budgets are shrinking, we must reset government so the American people are more free to increase economic opportunities and prosperity.

Rather than the Left's five pillars of a government-driven economy, America should return to President Ronald Reagan's four proven policies for an enduring economic recovery:

- real and sustained tax relief
- fiscal integrity
- smart regulatory reform
- sound monetary policy

Reagan trusted in Americans' entrepreneurial spirit, innovative talents, and industriousness, and he agreed with Adam Smith's insight that freedom and prosperity are inextricably entwined and mutually reinforcing.

But eternal vigilance is the price of our liberty and the prosperity it creates. If we are to remain the vanguard of free enterprise, we must overcome our current economic challenges.

The flexibility of our markets is endangered by excessive regulation, onerous litigation, and government redistribution of wealth. Special interests promote complex tax loopholes that impede the free flow of capital and divert it for less productive purposes, while the government is not adequately addressing the anxieties many citizens feel during globalization's era of rapid innovation and change. We must address the public's insecurities to prevent a backlash against the very free-enterprise system that is the foundation of our prosperity.

These developments and anxieties are neither recent nor temporary. They are the culmination of a generation of increased and excessive regulation; onerous and punitive tax policies; a lax emphasis on math and science education; unchecked and escalating health-care costs; rampant lawsuit abuse; arbitrary judicial decisions infringing on private property rights; an absence of an energy policy to meet our economic and security needs; the failure to fully enforce our rights and protections from unfair competition under international law and within the terms of present and potential trade agreements; the failure to expand the research-and-development capabilities that propel a high-powered economy; and the unconscionable acceptance of a welfare system that traps our fellow human beings in a soul-crushing cycle of dependence.

This is the cost of centrism: we have hamstrung our nation's people and innovative capabilities in the core areas of ideation, capitalization, production, distribution, and consumption. Our economy languishes, we possess fewer resources to meet national priorities, and our children will inherit fewer opportunities and a diminishing standard of living. Without effective action, one day America will cease to be the world's economic leader.

This is not inevitable. Although government has limited economic opportunities and growth through its intrusions into the marketplace, sovereign citizens retain the power to reject these detrimental policies and expand the scope of economic liberty. Yet time grows short. Other nations are preparing for the future. So must America. Achieving a humane, innovation-empowered economy in the twenty-first century requires enacting policies that will revitalize our prosperity by championing our economic liberty.

As has been the case throughout American history, this economic revitalization will be accomplished with private capital, by private initiative, and through the ingenuity and industriousness of our citizenry. Prosperity is created neither by government control nor by bureaucratic fiat. It is accomplished by free citizens acting in a free marketplace and freely choosing where their money is best spent, saved, and invested, and how resources are best valued and utilized; and by a skilled workforce prepared for productive and rewarding careers. Through these private exertions America has always been and will remain a land of innovative entrepreneurs, hardworking laborers, committed professionals, and the most productive industries.

It is imperative, then, that we build upon Reagan's four core policies for an enduring economic recovery by removing the numerous governmental roadblocks that obstruct economic development and deter investments from entrepreneurs here and abroad. Government must reject ill-intentioned and/or ill-conceived economic policies that lead to the Servile State. Instead, it must allow economic freedom to flourish, so citizens can thrive, create jobs, and build an exceptional, innovation-empowered American economy. Only this will reinvigorate the economy of our "shining city on a hill."

End "Too Big to Fail"

If the myth of "too big to fail" persists, America will repeat Japan's economically stagnant "lost decade," and our social upheavals will exponentially increase. "Too big to fail" must be ended, and reforms must be enacted that ensure a swift and certain "prepackaged" bankruptcy process for failing financial behemoths. This will prevent the dangerous concentrations of financial power that curtail entrepreneurial initiative, accountability, and transparency; foster a decentralized, competitive, and creative financial industry that will power an innovation economy; and reestablish that, in America, nothing is "too big to fail" except her sovereign people.

Tame the Taxman

Almost half of Americans do not pay income taxes. If the current system isn't reformed, a majority of Americans will consider income tax increases a boon, because they won't pay them and will receive the redistributed revenue. This is how the Left can replace free enterprise and property rights with class warfare and wealth redistribution as the warped foundation of America's economy. Compounding the problem, the tax code is too complex and punitive for the Americans paying income taxes to fully prosper. It discourages the economic initiative of entrepreneurs and workers, and diverts capital away from more profitable economic activities into shelters that reduce tax burdens.

The progressive income tax must be scrapped. In the interim, rates must be reduced across the board and simplified, and corporate and capital gains taxes must be lessened to stem further resource-allocation distortions that cost Americans jobs and new opportunities.

Fight for Fiscal Integrity

If you managed your family budget like Congress manages the federal budget, you wouldn't be reelected. You'd be incarcerated. Government spends what it takes; you spend what you make. The government pays for nothing, and taxpayers pay for everything. This has wrought big, broken, unaccountable government.

To stop out-of-control federal borrowing and spending and force government to honor its fiduciary duty to taxpayers, Congress must adhere to federalism and return power to those governmental units closest to the people; implement spending caps that prevent the federal budget from growing faster than a family's budget; pass a legislative line-item veto to end pork-barrel earmarks; attach sunset provisions to new legislation; enact entitlement reforms that implement market reforms for cost savings and that empower recipients rather than expand the federal bureaucracy; and send the states a constitutional balanced-budget amendment to adopt. If Congress refuses, sovereign citizens have a certain remedy: vote out spendthrift politicians on Election Day.

Cut the Red Tape Worm

Government red tape is akin to an eight-track tape: it's outdated and nobody digs it. The arbitrary, unrealistic, impractical, and unnecessary rules and regulations that a largely unaccountable federal bureaucracy places upon American entrepreneurs are like a red tape worm sapping our economy of the liquidity and flexibility needed to compete in the global marketplace.

To reignite American enterprise, regulatory reform must keep government from intruding into the marketplace beyond its legitimate mandate to protect against monopoly, fraud, abuse of power, and crime; must provide for essential services and basic infrastructure; and must foster an environment in which parties can efficiently and safely contract and carry out exchanges. This will enable businesses to thrive and create jobs.

No Trespassing

In our constitutional free republic, where government was established to protect citizens' lives and property, our private property rights and political rights are indivisible and reinforcing. There can be no exceptions. Americans have earned the fruits of their labors and own them. They are not on loan from a socialist state. This is lost upon federal regulators and judicial activists.

A glaring instance of gutting private property rights occurred on June 5, 2000, when a divided United States Supreme Court issued its *Kelo v. City of New London* decision, which ruled that government (in this case municipalities) could use its power of eminent domain to take citizens' homes and real property and transfer it to private entities for economic development. In support of this decision, Justice John Paul Stevens opined that "promoting economic development is a traditional and long-accepted function of government." He forgot the government was first and foremost established to protect citizens' lives and property.

To Stevens, government knows best. He wrote: "*The city* has carefully formulated an economic development that it believes will provide appreciable benefits to the community, including—but by no means limited to— new jobs and *increased tax revenue* [emphasis added]." In Stevens's world, like Rousseau's, property rights are mere public privileges granted or terminated by government. A well-heeled lawyer who filed a brief on behalf of New London reflected the same worldview when he argued that, had the case been won by the homeowners, "it would greatly limit what cities and towns all over the country could do."

In her dissent, Justice Sandra Day O'Connor pointed out how misguided such thinking is: "The specter of condemnation hangs over all property. . . . The government now has license to transfer property from those with fewer resources to those with more. . . . The Founders cannot have intended this perverse result."

Homeowners across America were justly outraged that their appointed servants on the courts disregarded Sir Edward Coke's dictum that cases must be decided according to "the golden and straight metwand of the law, and not to the incertain and crooked cord of discretion."

Now the battle to curtail the regulatory power of bureaucrats to encroach on private property rights must be fought legislatively. A constitutional amendment must be adopted that reaffirms citizens' private property against state usurpation.

And real property is not the only area where we must be vigilant against federal infringement on our property and liberty. The very same legislative and bureaucratic means the government uses to capriciously curtail our property rights are combining with proposed "international agreements" to assault our Second Amendment rights. This constitutes an unjustifiable attempt to diminish our God-given rights to gun ownership and self-defense by the very government that was established to defend those rights and all others. Thus, Americans' Second Amendment rights must be fully accorded their express constitutional protections from federal encroachment. Any international agreement impairing these rights must be rejected as a reduction of our liberty, sovereignty, and property.

Cure Health Care
The Left has defied the consent of the governed to foist the foundations of a government-run, bureaucrat-dictated medicine upon Americans. As Dr. David Janda, M.D., has warned, the premise of this execrable law is that government can reduce and ration the supply of health care to "control" costs. This is absurd. Per the law of supply and demand, if the government reduces the supply of health care while the demand for it increases from demographic pressures and medical advances, the costs will spiral upward, and the government will increasingly intrude into your personal decisions and savings.

Americans deserve free-market, patient-centered wellness that leverages the communications revolution and market forces to increase the supply of health care so it can meet the rising demand, reduce costs, and expand access.

Immediate, obvious measures include:

- reforming medical liability laws
- ending exclusions for preexisting conditions
- expanding Health Savings Accounts
- providing tax credits for purchasing private health insurance
- allowing Association Health Plans
- permitting health insurance purchases across state lines
- encouraging individuals to insure against changes in health status
- incentivizing preventative health care
- applying information technology to enhance transparency and increase efficiencies

Further, for the less fortunate and most vulnerable among us, Federally Qualified Health Clinics (FQHC) can be expanded; doctors and other health-care professionals can be incentivized to provide their services at these clinics for either immediate or future considerations; and a "Project Navigator" program attached to each FQHC can assist the underserved in accessing the health-care system.

Finally, people suffering from "orphan diseases"— rare afflictions requiring a lifetime of special care— should be compassionately assisted through our nation's social safety net.

By empowering consumers and freeing the supply of health care to expand through increased competition, experimentation, and innovation in health-care technology and delivery, we can stabilize—not socialize—health-care costs and nurture a vigorous, well-capitalized, competitive market that will deliver the optimum solutions for Americans' wellness within the best health-care system in the world.

Case Closed

Justice is blind; she isn't a lottery. We must restore equity, surety, and sanity to our legal system. When Congress is compelled to pass legislation ensuring that food companies, distributors, and restaurants are not liable for someone eating too many cheeseburgers, we are nearing the day when very few entrepreneurs will dare make or sell goods or provide services (even charitable ones) for fear of being bankrupted by frivolous lawsuits. True tort reform that promotes the moral and legal principle of personal responsibility for one's actions, limits economic and non-economic damages, implements a "loser pays" rule, and punishes frivolous lawsuits will free entrepreneurs to promote prosperity and job creation.

Maximum American Energy

Energy powers our economy. We need to continue seeking reliable, cost-efficient sources of energy through a market-based plan that contains three key components: maximum energy production, commonsense conservation, and free-market, green innovations. Recognizing that America's greatest resource is her free people, this "all of the above" energy plan will provide maximum American energy and responsibly transition America from fossil fuels to alternative energies.

Capital Ideas

We must continue our distinguished history of producing and attracting private capital and private-sector research institutions that spur the innovations fueling economic growth. To do so, especially in the areas of research and development, we must enact an appropriate period for protecting intellectual-property rights and patents before they enter the public domain, and effectively enforce intellectual-property and patent laws domestically and internationally. Absent the confidence that their ideas will be protected, investors and innovators will not take the financial and personal risks needed to develop new ideas.

To foster an innovation-empowered economy, we must encourage investment in our economy through lower corporate and capital gains taxation, and low regulatory barriers to the commercialization of new ideas, processes, and products. Eliminating government-imposed barriers will inspire and attract the intellects and capital needed to keep America the world's premier innovator—not a dependent importer.

Return Learning to Education

Our educational system has provided preceding generations of Americans with the tools to pursue and attain their aspirations. More than ever, students need a broad education, not a narrow indoctrination. Parents must fulfill their primary role in a child's moral education, and teachers must fulfill their primary role in a child's educational development. Federal bureaucrats must not usurp or impair the roles of parents and teachers.

Consequently, we must reverse the increasing federal control over education, including any attempts to discriminate against charter schools and home schooling. Our children must be grounded in academic fundamentals, such as reading, math, and science; become familiar with technology; and experience a comprehensive core curriculum which empowers them with the cognitive abilities to independently think, innovate, and thrive within the economy of the future. And, most importantly, our children should be imbued with a lifelong love of learning.

Secure Citizens' Sovereignty and Soil

Big government, big business, and the Left have combined to cheat us of our sovereignty and tax money by enticing and exploiting illegal immigrants in America. This crisis mocks the sacrifices and concerns of naturalized citizens and legal immigrants. But we must not blame the illegal immigrants, the vast majority of whom are honest, industrious exiles fleeing tyranny and poverty to live in liberty and prosperity. Without animus or amnesty, we must solve this untenable crisis by reversing the core problems that have caused it.

First and foremost, we must secure our borders, especially in this time of war against a terrorist enemy that has already struck us on our own soil.

Second, we must punish businesses that "cheat to compete" by employing illegal workers; unions that refuse to report illegal workers on job sites and within their memberships; and state and local governments that flout federal immigration laws by establishing "sanctuary cities."

Third, we must stop providing taxpayers' money to illegal immigrants.

Fourth, we must make clear there that will be no amnesty now or ever for illegal immigrants.

Finally, we must fix the entire broken system of legal immigration by returning to the principles of asylum for and the assimilation of new immigrants, including the adoption of English as America's official language—for the benefit of both immigrants and citizens—and by logically differentiating rural enterprises from other enterprises in granting work visas.

Responsibly and justly ending illegal immigration will secure our sovereignty and soil, and keep America a beacon of liberty and hope for the world's tired, poor, and huddled masses.

Freedom Trade

Despite arguments for "free trade" and "protectionism," negotiated trade is the reality. We must pursue *freedom trade*: fair trade with free nations on the most advantageous terms possible. We must no longer enrich unfriendly regimes at our own expense.

Freedom trade restores the link between American trade, national security, and human rights. Freedom trade agreements must guarantee reciprocity of opportunity in open markets—that is, a trading partner must treat our exports the same as those of every other nation and not unfairly subsidize their own exports to our nation or any other. This requires agreements that equalize tax rates, balance tariffs, and prevent currency manipulation and the subsidization of exports, because such measures are economically inefficient, unjustly penalize specific producer groups within trading partners, and exacerbate tensions between nations. It further requires full compliance with international norms pertaining to the protection of intellectual property and open markets. In accordance with America's storied role in spreading freedom and free enterprise to the world, freedom trade will expand Americans' prosperity and promote our security.

Solidarity for Prosperity

America can no longer afford an adversarial relationship between management and labor. There must be a more orderly and equitable process of resolving disputes short of strikes and/or outsourcing. This "fair broker" role was posited and practiced by President Theodore Roosevelt, who forthrightly confronted the fact that neither business nor labor was always right: "Corporations and labor-unions are alike bound to serve the commonwealth . . . and this can only come as the result of the state becoming the partner of both, a partner sincerely anxious to help both, but determined that each shall do its duty."

It is time for a new set of ground rules for the interaction between business and labor, one they jointly determine and then present to Congress for its review and potential approval. While many fervently argue that such a conciliatory role for government is presently impossible, the only president of an AFL-CIO affiliated union who reached our nation's highest office—Ronald Reagan—disagreed:

> Unions represent some of the freest institutions in this land. Too often, discussions about the labor

movement dwell only on disputes or corruption or strikes. . . . It also might be nice for once if we could hear about the thousands of hard-working, honest, union officials who have done so much to improve your movement and raise the standard of living for all Americans. . . . [So] instead of workers and management trying to solve the dilemma . . . by opposing each other, it's time you joined forces . . . so you can get on with the task of rebuilding our economy. Saving American jobs and raising the standard of living for all our people—that's part of the job.

Green Main Street

Successful conservation relies upon individuals and families; voluntary, community-based initiatives; and market-oriented encouragements of entrepreneurial innovations for green technologies, such as broad research-and-development tax credits for companies and income-tax deductions for users. We must leave sound public land-use statutes in place and build upon them through community- and market-based conservation initiatives, including property-tax relief for sustainable developments and income-tax deductions for homeowners who increase their energy efficiencies. These steps will prevent the government from pursuing politically motivated, scientifically unsound policies that infringe upon property rights and preclude the prosperity that enables developing nations to lead in environmental protection. Only this approach can inspire and optimize the ideas and innovations brought forward by our nation's greatest force for conservation—her people—and ensure a purer earth for future generations.

Emancipate the Poor

We are a moral people and virtuous community—one that, with the consent of the governed, provides a social safety net to "help those who cannot help themselves" so, where possible, they can regain the dignity of self-reliance and begin or renew their pursuit of the American Dream. But Americans' compassion has been grotesquely abused by big government, and our poor remain chained to a soul-crushing cycle of government dependence. To emancipate the poor, we must innovatively implement ownership principles within individually and community targeted empowerment programs. This necessitates ending the monstrous top-down, bureaucratic approach to welfare and replacing it with grassroots, bottom-up initiatives that foster an independent and entrepreneurial culture among the impoverished, based upon their freedom and dignity, private property, and free enterprise.

The guiding principle for emancipating the poor, which instructed much of the late Jack Kemp's "progressive conservatism," is subsidiarity: the smallest unit capable of solving a problem must not be prevented from doing so. Every federal assistance program must be scrutinized and either restructured or scrapped in accordance with this principle. The result will be an increase of self-reliance and a reduction of wasteful, injurious federal spending.

Again, the humane goal is to provide participants the dignity of independent and productive living. For as Robert Nisbet observed, absent "a clear sense of cultural purpose, membership, status and continuity . . . no amount of mere material welfare will serve to arrest the developing sense of alienation in our society." We must nurture the poor's inherent dignity and capacity for self-government so they can seize their American Dream.

Americans Are Patriots, Not Materialists

Our free-market prosperity is founded upon a virtuous culture. It stems from free people engaged in free enterprise in free markets with private property rights—all protected by the rule of law. This economic growth is not an end unto itself; its chief importance lies in the fact that it empowers Americans to pursue happiness within their families, their communities, and our country.

During our age of globalization, as corporations become "virtual" and reduce the traditional terms of employment, such as pensions and benefits; as intermediating institutions wither under statist attack and reduced leisure time; and as the full force of globalization encroaches upon Americans' cherished way of life and necessitates the painful restructuring of family and business budgets and practices, the state will increase its efforts to tempt individuals into embracing its false promises of economic security. Standing in the shadows of the Servile State, we face a stark choice: liberty and prosperity, or servility and stagnation.

To choose wisely, we should be guided by two unexpected compatriots in the struggle for a humane American and global economy—Robert Kennedy and Ronald Reagan.

In a 1968 speech in Detroit shortly before his assassination, Senator Kennedy implored Americans to discard statistical measurements of material gratification and instead embrace the moral dimensions of a humane economy:

> We will find neither national purpose nor personal satisfaction in a mere continuation of economic progress, in an endless amassing of worldly goods. We cannot measure national spirit by the Dow-Jones average, nor national achievement by the gross national product.... It does not allow for the health of our families, the quality of their education or the joy of their play. It is indifferent to the decency of our factories and the safety of our streets alike. It does not include the beauty of our poetry or the strength of our marriages, the intelligence of our public debate or the integrity of our public officials. It allows neither for the justice of our courts, nor for the justness of our dealings with each other. The gross national product measures neither our wit nor our courage, neither our wisdom nor our learning, neither our compassion nor our devotion to country. It measures everything, in short, except that which makes life worthwhile; and it can tell us everything about America—except whether we are proud to be Americans.

Proud Americans have the moral courage to defend their freedoms from the impending Servile State. They will not acquiesce as their servant government claims that it is a "necessary evil" to unfairly use taxpayer dollars to protect the interests of a few financiers, when doing so undermines the fundamental workings of our free-market system. Americans will not run scared into the state's icy embrace and squander their God-given freedom upon illusory government security. As at other challenging times, Americans are patriots, not materialists.

In 1982, nearly fourteen years after his death, Senator Kennedy's view of a more humane economy was embraced by a man who restored Americans' trust in their political and financial institutions, because he trusted the people. That man was President Ronald Reagan, who at the Conservative Political Action Conference declared:

> Higher productivity, a larger gross national product, a healthy Dow Jones average—they are our goals and are worthy ones. But our real concerns are not statistical goals or material gain. We want to expand personal freedom, to renew the American dream for every American. We seek to restore opportunity and reward, to value again personal achievement and individual excellence. We seek to rely on the ingenuity and energy of the American people to better their own lives and those of millions of other around the world.

Within the legacies of these great and good men lies the moral foundation for a rejuvenated culture and economy. Our current course, and big government itself, is unsustainable in this age of globalization and innovation. We must resist the Servile State's evanescent succor in "economic security," and fight through the darkest depths to the distant shore of hope—a hope William Wordsworth expressed in verse: "Then a wish, / My best and favorite aspiration, mounts / With yearning toward some philosophic song / Of Truth that cherishes our daily life."

Cherishing our way of life, we realize that America is a delicate mosaic of honest, hardworking, and loving people pursuing their dreams. From their brows falls the salt of our earth; from their hands springs American prosperity. Advancing economic freedom empowers the majestic American people to lead an economic renaissance that keeps our nation the world's economic engine; to forge a humane, innovation-empowered economy in harmony with our transformational times; and to show the world what a free people can achieve.

4

WIN OUR WAR FOR FREEDOM

"Against All Enemies"

In 2006 I attended my oldest son's eighth-grade gradua-
tion. Graduating with him was a girl named Jennifer, the
daughter of my childhood friend Miles, who was absent.
That night, I talked with his wife, Karen, who told me how
painful it was for their family to have Miles so abruptly
deployed to Iraq.

I did not try to comfort Karen by saying that her
husband was in Iraq defending global stability or United
Nations resolutions. I thanked Karen for her family's sacrifice, because Miles was in Iraq honoring his solemn pledge
to God and to us to "support and defend the Constitution
of the United States against all enemies."

Unlike Miles, many had somehow dismissed or denigrated the danger we face.

On September 11, 2001, our nation was invaded, three

thousand of our fellow Americans were murdered, and we were thrust into an unsought struggle—the War for Freedom—against the butcher bin Laden's death cult and Middle Eastern fascism. It was a hard truth told anew: As the world's beacon of freedom and bastion of hope for the enslaved and oppressed, America remains the target for every tyrant and terrorist bent upon conquest. Frankly, the enemy lusts to kill us for our "sin" of being free.

As the attacked, we do not primarily wage a War *on* Terrorism. We wage a War *for* Freedom. Our immediate enemy is "infidel fascism"; our long-term enemy is Iranian imperialism. Against the terrorists—for the liberty of generations unborn—we must reinstitute President Ronald Reagan's successful strategy against the Soviets: "We win; they lose."

Right now, in Afghanistan, Pakistan, and Iraq, and throughout the world, humanity is battling infidel fascism. In Islam, *kufar* means "infidels." Because al-Qaeda and bin Laden butcher innocents, including Muslims, they are the *kufar* who pervert Islam's peaceful path and sinfully seek to enslave others of God's children. Intensifying the threat, the enemy is also fascist. This hideous ideological concoction has cunningly adapted to a globalized world: it is well organized, media savvy, and technologically adept—and willing to kill its own children to kill ours. We confront this faceless foe along a million-mile front. This is global gangsterism—a moral cancer to be scourged from our world.

Among traditional nation-states, Iran is our most clear, present, and pressing danger. Through a marriage of convenience with Sunni-led infidel fascism, Shiia-ruled Iranian imperialism is complicit in spreading terrorism—

often with the aid and comfort of Syria, with which the Iranians have signed a "mutual defense" treaty, one akin to the meeting of the bloody-minded that was 1939's Russo-German Molotov-Ribbentrop Pact.

Governed by a radical Islamic politburo of mullahs, Iran exports its revolution through terrorism and intimidation, including the arming and shielding of our enemies in Iraq, and the regime's defiant development and proliferation of nuclear weapons. Iran and Syria are key financiers and kindred spirits to the terror organizations that control the Palestinian Authority and seek to destabilize Lebanon. Fanatically committed, these Iranian imperialists and their ideological soul mates and economic patrons are underestimated or ignored at the world's peril.

We must unite as the latest generation of Americans duty-bound to defend freedom in an hour of maximum danger. Courageous and committed, we must affirm our full measure of devotion to our troops, their families, and an American and allied victory.

The foundation of our victory strategy is the principle that our free people have historically and heroically championed to defeat our enemies: To ensure liberty for ourselves, we must aid the extension of liberty to those attacked and/or enslaved by our mutual enemies. Therefore, to retreat in the face of the al-Qaeda death cult's fanaticism and Mideast fascism would betray our revolutionary commitment to and inherited legacy of liberty. To retreat in the face of the enemy now would morally disarm us and turn the region's people from us and toward the enemy. And to retreat in the face of the enemy now would dishonor the American and Coalition citizen-soldiers striving to defend our nations and emancipate millions of Muslims from subjugation so our world can reap new blessings of freedom. While these new blessings of freedom seem closer at hand since President Obama declared the end of active combat operations in Iraq, we must not slacken our grip on the terrorist enemy, which remains obsessed with our destruction.

Thus, our course remains tough, but our cause is just. Our enemy is the sire of tyranny; we are the children of liberty. We cannot coexist, as the enemy propagandizes and murderously proves. With prudence, purpose, and an understanding of history, we must prove that our devotion to liberty transcends our enemy's obsession with death. United as a nation and with other free peoples, we must never retreat. For once again ambushed but unbowed, we heirs of liberty must defeat these latest enemies and, for the sake of generations yet unnamed, walk and widen the path of human freedom.

The first step is to retain our moral clarity and never forget the following truths in our nation's War for Freedom.

Ten Truths of Our War for Freedom

1. America is not engaged in a War on Terror. America is engaged in a War for Freedom. Our duty began with our liberty on July 4, 1776, and every American generation must fulfill its duty in the struggle against tyranny.
2. Afghanistan and Iraq were never separate wars; they have always been battle theaters in the War for Freedom.

3. Our terrorist enemy is not novel. America has previously defeated enemies ranging from sword-wielding pirates to nuclear-armed nations. We will again.

4. Like the Communist North Vietnamese, this enemy knows that it cannot defeat our military on the battlefield, so it creates carnage and chaos to persuade the American public to withdraw our troops from the battlefield. In sum: the enemy is employing violence in an act of psychological warfare.

5. To win this struggle, America must maintain its moral clarity, cognizant that the enemy is evil and we are emancipators.

6. The enemy is avowedly imperialist; America is demonstrably a liberator. To safeguard our own freedom, we have extended freedom to more than fifty million Muslims.

7. Whoever doubts our beneficent intentions should be reminded that Paris is a foreign capital, not a state capital.

8. We must reaffirm that the United States will never abandon a sovereign democracy that is under terrorist attack.

9. We must undertake a policy of constructive containment, which circles imperial nations with democracies until these tyrannies implode beneath their own peoples' desire to be free.

10. Where the enemy threatens to establish bases of operations, we must aid in building sustainable community institutions through prudent and localized development and reconstruction, foster-

ing the societal stability needed to prevent troubled states from becoming failed states and havens for terrorism.

Our Moral Foundation in the War for Freedom

Abstract strategic imperatives are insufficient rationales for Americans to wage war. As a civilized people, we will fight only a "just war," defined as one necessarily engaged and morally waged.

While healthy debates will occur over the proper means of prosecuting our unsought War for Freedom against terrorism, America and her allies must remember that we hold the moral high ground. America and her allies are necessarily defending themselves against terrorists and their state sponsors in a war which has already murdered thousands of innocent citizens. The practitioners and sponsors of terrorism have placed themselves outside the community of moral nations. Free nations have allied to end terrorism and end the state sponsorship of terrorism, for until the terrorists and their state sponsors are defeated, we remain in peril.

We not only have the moral right to defend ourselves and defeat our enemies; we have the moral duty to do no less. It remains as President Franklin Roosevelt explained in another day of maximal danger: "Freedom means the supremacy of human rights everywhere. Our support goes to those who struggle to gain those rights or keep them. Our strength is our unity of purpose."

Presently, such unity of martial and moral purpose is being fulfilled by helping the newly liberated peoples of Afghanistan and Iraq transition into democratic Middle Eastern allies in the world's War for Freedom. The past is prologue. The eternal truth that won World War II and the Cold War will win our global War for Freedom: all human beings have a God-given right to liberty and justice that no person or power can deny.

Helping to reconstruct these newly freed nations is a protracted and excruciating task. But if our nation really believes that all human beings are equally God's children, whether they be free or yearn to breathe free, one cannot, after a cruel sip of hope, condemn millions of God's equally beloved children to a saturnalia of slaughter. If we and our allies abandon these souls, it will reveal a callow contentment with our own liberty and a calloused apathy to others' enslavement. And it will increase our own danger, as President Kennedy warned: "If we do not meet our commitments to [West] Berlin, where later will we stand?"

Our Holistic Strategy for Unconditional Victory

As in all our past trials by fire, today the United States must reaffirm its commitment to the expansion of human freedom. Eliminating terrorists and their state sponsors is not the sole goal of our effort. In this necessary self-defense of our freedom we also will liberate the human beings suffering under these tyrants' oppression. This is in keeping with our history as a nation built on the clarion vision of a more hopeful, peaceful, and prosperous life for oppressed peoples and, most importantly, the self-evident truth that all human beings are endowed by their Creator with the inalienable rights to life, liberty, and the pursuit of happiness.

In active theaters of war, therefore, America and her allies must unleash and infuse liberty throughout counter-insurgency operations and concomitant "bottom-up" reconstruction efforts. This strategy incorporates two fundamental principles: (1) a democratic society evolves upward from its traditional roots of order, not down from a centralized bureaucratic government, and (2) a nation's transformation into a liberal democracy must contemporaneously provide transactional benefits to its citizens. This bottom-up strategy will empower newly emancipated peoples to shape their own destinies, join our family of free nations, and, together, help all humanity defeat infidel fascism.

First, this strategy, which must be implemented in an active theater of war against a guerilla enemy, requires cooperatively strengthening the indigenous population's national and local security forces to permit the "breathing room" for a local political shift away from an insurgency and toward liberty. This separation of the population from the enemy will be the foundation upon which is built a stable and free nation that starts capturing terrorists instead of supporting them.

Second, most of a terrorized indigenous population will refuse to risk their own or their loved ones' lives for the long-repressed goods of liberty and equality. The newly freed must experience how their political enfranchisement results in concrete benefits to their lives, including improvements in their personal security; their water, sewage, and electricity infrastructure; and good governance in general. Thus, America and allies must use diplomatic, economic, and, where necessary, martial resources—starting at the local level—to help the newly elected governments match democracy's electoral ideals with palpable benefits, so the population can embrace and build upon their freedom.

We saw the importance of a bottom-up or "local reconciliation" counterinsurgency strategy in Iraq. In his September 7, 2007, letter to the Multi-National Force Iraq, General David Petraeus stressed the need for such a program as he described the Iraqis' local political shift to liberty:

> While this concept is playing out differently in various areas across Iraq, it is grounded in a desire shared by increasing numbers of Iraqis—to oppose extremist elements and their ideologies. This is very significant because, as many of you know first hand, extremists cannot survive without the support of the population. The popular rejection of al-Qaeda and its ideology has, for example, helped transform Anbar Province this year from one of the most dangerous areas of Iraq to one of the safest. The popular rejection of extremists has helped Coalition and Iraqi Forces take away other areas from al-Qaeda as well, and we are seeing a spread of this sentiment in an ever-increasing number of Sunni areas. Now, in fact, we are also seeing a desire to reject extremists emerge in many Shiia areas.

Three years later, General Petraeus was leading America and her allies' efforts in embattled Afghanistan, but by that point his vision was being realized in Iraq. Security increases allowed local reconciliation to strengthen Iraqi participation in their security and hastened the day that they would be solely responsible for it. Thus, as in the early days of American independence, Iraqi local reconciliation preceded and facilitated national reconciliation. It signaled our victory in liberating Iraq and pointed the way to victory in liberating Afghanistan.

Employing diplomatic and economic reconstruction measures, the bottom-up Petraeus counterinsurgency model in active theaters of war can be adapted to prevent ungoverned regions and struggling states from becoming failed or rogue states and harbors for *kufar* fascism. This prescient reconstruction will emphasize the creation of localized, sustainable democratic and economic institutions that increase liberty, prosperity, health, and the rule of law among the indigenous population.

Further, American citizens with ancestral ties to the nation in question and willing to volunteer should be employed to interface with the local population and assist in the development of these institutions.

Finally, on a national reconstruction level, the United States should work with the host nation to identify projects that bring the greatest increase in the population's quality of life.

The goal, of course, is to help the indigenous population realize that the United States is not an imperial enemy but a loyal ally committed to helping expand the blessings of liberty and prosperity.

Liberty Lights the Way

In our War for Freedom against terrorism, America and her allies are following the core principles of President Reagan's Cold War victory strategy. As with his predecessors from President Harry Truman onward, in the cause of victory over Communism President Reagan's every action was informed by one unshakable, self-evident truth: human beings want their God-given right to freedom.

This truth informed every strategic move he made, and led to the emancipation of the Eastern European nations trapped as satellites of the Soviet empire. Once these captive peoples were free, it was but a matter of time until the Soviet Union's oppressed people demanded their liberty and America's nuclear-armed enemy peacefully imploded.

Today, liberty is as lethal to Iranian imperialism as it was to Soviet Communism. America and her allies must lead the effort to isolate and implode the Iranian regime by preventing the regime from obtaining a nuclear weapon; imposing economic and diplomatic sanctions; supporting the Iranian people's "Green Revolution"; and freeing the peoples of new democracies on Iran's borders. This strategy alone will ensure that the mullahs' despotic, terror-sponsoring regime will join the Soviet Union in the trash can of history.

Critically, there is one distinction: Iran must never be allowed to develop a nuclear weapon—period. If diplomatic measures prove unsuccessful, the Iranian nuclear program must be stopped by the United States and/or her allies. There is no other sane or safe course of action.

Unfortunately, this is disputed by the two members of the UN's Permanent Security Council who happen to be the ringleaders of the mutual-security group the Shanghai Cooperation Organization (SCO): Communist China and Putin's Russia. Despite more than a decade of U.S. protestations, China and Russia are the top exporters of nuclear technology, chemical weapons precursors, and guided missiles to Iran, to which the SCO granted formal observer status in 2005. (In the same year, the United States sought this status but was denied by the SCO.) In 2004 the U.S.-China Economic and Security Review Commission (USCC) declared that "Chinese entities continue to assist Iran with dual-use missile-related items, raw materials and chemical weapons-related production equipment and technology." The USCC further noted that these transfers took place after the Communist Chinese government's 2003 pledge to withhold missile technology from the Iranian regime. Such assistance also comes from Communist China's client state North Korea, which is used to tie down and diminish American interests in Asia.

With this relationship, Communist China and Putin's Russia use Iran to reduce America's strategic interests in the Middle East. In return, Iran hopes to thwart America's attempts to isolate the rogue regime and frustrate its nuclear ambitions. The enabling of Iran will persist until Communist China and Putin's Russia are persuaded that continued instability in the Middle East is as damaging to their interests as it is to the interests of the United States and the West. In a diplomatic task that will be as difficult as it is necessary, the United States and Europe must unite to link all facets of their relationships with Communist China and Putin's Russia for the cessation of nuclear proliferation by Iran and North Korea.

On a critical final note, the United States' success in the War for Freedom is inextricably linked to the survival and success of her democratic, stalwart ally Israel. Daily subjected to murderous terrorist attacks and Iranian nuclear threats of a "second Holocaust," Israel courageously perseveres in the face of its enemies' threats and in its strategic friendship with the United States. If America turns her back on Israel under the delusion that this will solve the Middle East's travails, all hope for true peace in the region will die along with our nation's honor. The United States should encourage a mutually beneficial accord between Israel and the Palestinians but should never endeavor to dictate the terms of that peace. Otherwise the latest road to hell will be paved with the good intentions that once gave Czechoslovakia to the barbarians in the vain hope for "peace in our time."

"Salvation Will Not Be Denied Us"

Waging and winning the War for Freedom requires the arduous eradication of terrorists around the globe through diplomatic, economic, and military initiatives in tiered theaters of operations. There is no retreat in this unsought struggle.

In his December 26, 1941, address to a joint session of Congress, Prime Minister Winston Churchill implored another shocked generation of Americans sucked into a world conflagration to firmly press on:

> Some people may be startled or momentarily depressed when, like your President, I speak of a long

and hard war. But our peoples would rather know the truth, somber though it be. And, after all, when we are doing the noblest work in the world, not only defending our hearths and homes but the cause of freedom in other lands. . . . Sure I am that this day—now we are the masters of our fate; that the task which has been set us is not above our strength; that its pangs and toils are not beyond our endurance. As long as we have faith in our cause and an unconquerable will-power, salvation will not be denied us.

We are again targeted by tyrants and terrorists who know they cannot enslave humanity so long as America and her allies breathe free. And again, salvation will not be denied us.

Protect Our Hearths and Homes

Given the nature of our enemy and our globalized, interconnected world, we face unprecedented constraints on our nation's ability to broadcast to the American people our victories in the War for Freedom. Touting victories has been a key factor in wars—used to galvanize the home front and demoralize the enemy. But now the United States and her allies cannot list all of the terrorist attacks prevented without jeopardizing precious (and often scarce) intelligence sources or instructing terrorists as to how our homeland defense operates. The American public is reduced to accepting the proposition that "no news is good news."

Because Americans rarely hear of our wins, there arises a conundrum: the more successful the efforts to stop terrorist attacks on American soil, the more likely it is that Americans will believe the war has been won or the threat significantly diminished. And because our enemy rarely hears of its defeats, terrorists can continue deluding themselves that they are winning.

Exacerbating and entwined with the "no news is good news" conundrum is the "man bites dog" dictum of journalism, which fosters a barrage of reports about America's missteps in our War for Freedom. Such reporting has crafted an inaccurate public perception of America's overall success in the war effort. This public perception is demonstrably erroneous, but Americans who have heard no news or are bombarded by negative news are not easily cured of this conceit.

The general public's perception of the threat is also assaulted by a far more insidious vision of the War for Freedom—namely, that it is an overblown threat far less important than "climate change." Incredibly, the Left's eco-warriors are trying to supplant the real global war with a phony battle against global warming.

Two vignettes should suffice to prove this. First, for his efforts to stop productive people from waging biocide against Goddess Gaia, artiste Al Gore won the Nobel *Peace* Prize. Second, on the cover of its April 2008 edition, *Time* magazine Photoshopped the famous World War II picture of the Marines on Iwo Jima. This time, they weren't hoisting a flag; they were hoisting a tree. Such an affront to our veterans and our history evinces the Left's insistence on ignoring the fact that on September 11, 2001, three thousand

American souls were exterminated by al-Qaeda's fanatics, not by Al Gore's fantasies. Grudgingly, we must grant Sartre his due: the Left's world is, indeed, absurd. In its obsession with biocide, the Left would drive the West to suicide.

In his book *Unholy Alliance*, former radical leftist David Horowitz explains why:

> New Leftists viewed America as an imperialist state, the guardian of a global system that plundered the poor. Their politics was distinguished by its warm embrace of the Stalinist regimes in Cuba and North Vietnam, and by its "critical support" (its own term of choice) for the Soviet bloc that . . . it regarded as a check on the imperial ambitions of the United States.

The Left's inveterate ideological need to "blame America first" has persisted throughout our War for Freedom against terrorism, including our attempts to secure our homeland.

For all of these reasons, we confront dangerous fallacies that diminish Americans' homeland security efforts. These fallacies include the assertion that Americans have no real need for homeland security, because there have been no new attacks since September 11, 2001; that homeland security can be achieved by focusing on instruments of potential terror rather than individual terrorists; that technology alone can secure our borders against our enemies; and that terrorism can be considered a wholly criminal matter.

These fallacies must be disabused by this sage advice: Know your enemy.

Knowing our enemy will allow us often to anticipate and prevent its plans, targets, and tactics. But to fully stop the enemy's attacks requires hard intelligence in real time through vital tools such as the Foreign Intelligence Surveillance Act (FISA), which must not be weakened, lest we lose one fateful step to the enemy's assassins. It also necessitates national preparedness, including expanded emergency planning and training first responders, and the enhancement of cyber-security measures to foil new attacks. We must implement a risk-based analysis to determine most accurately which sites the terrorists will target, what tools they may use in their targeting of these sites, and what new technologies must be devised to counter the enemy's threat.

Finally, we must advance the partnership between the public sector and the private sector in developing and using homeland security pilot programs. We must properly weigh the interests of security and liberty, realizing that the enemy targets both, and reject the temptation to equate more spending and bureaucracy with promoting homeland security—more is not always better.

"We Will Do No Less"

On September 11, 2001, we suffered our most grievous wound on our soil. Our fellow citizens were murdered by butchers willing to kill themselves and their children to kill us. Those horrible acts remind us why we must stop future attacks in their earliest stage.

This grim acceptance of our sacred duty was embodied and expressed by our valiant, wartime commander in chief:

There has now come a time when you and I must see the cold, inexorable necessity of saying to these inhuman, unrestrained seekers of world conquest and permanent world domination by the sword: "You seek to throw our children and our children's children into your form of terrorism and slavery. You have now attacked our own safety. You shall go no further." . . .

The American people have faced other grave crises in their history—with American courage, and with American resolution. They will do no less today.

They know the actualities of the attacks upon us. They know the necessities of a bold defense against these attacks. They know that the times call for clear heads and fearless hearts.

And with that inner strength that comes to a free people conscious of their duty, and conscious of the righteousness of what they do, they will—with Divine help and guidance—stand their ground against this latest assault upon their democracy, their sovereignty, and their freedom.

The wartime leader who made those remarks was President Franklin Delano Roosevelt, addressing the nation in a fireside chat on September 11, 1941.

The American people faced down the crisis of which FDR spoke. We will do no less today.

Bind Their Wounds and Tend Their Hopes

17 November 2006

Dear Grandma,

Thank you very much for both your continued support and the prayers that I know you are sending up on my behalf. . . . I hope that your Thanksgiving will be delightful and the family will have a memorable experience, in a good way. . . . Everything here is working out well, because I know that I have a caring family behind me. I will be home soon, already almost two months have passed and April will be here soon. Take care of yourselves and let that wrist of yours heal. I love you and miss seeing you and Grandpa.

Take Care,
Mark

On January 25, 2007, at a checkpoint between Fallujah and Baghdad, Iraq, Marine Corporal Mark D. Kidd, twenty-six years young, was killed in action.

In our War for Freedom, out of respect for the ultimate sacrifices of Mark and all the fallen of this "Greatest Generation," let us bind the wounds and tend the hopes of their comrades-in-arms we are blessed to welcome home. After all, if not for the contributions and sacrifices of the men and women of our military, America would not still be the world's exemplar of freedom and democracy. Throughout our great history, these brave individuals have answered the call to defend our freedoms without hesitation or concern for the personal sacrifices they were certain to endure. This is a debt we can never fully repay.

Sadly, however, too often when America's veterans and their families turn to their government for help and care, they encounter a massive, faceless bureaucracy that is excruciatingly slow to serve them. This is unacceptable.

First, we must take care of our veterans' health care. Examinations and interviews need to be improved to ensure that our troops are not suffering latent injuries, including traumatic brain injuries, post-traumatic stress disorder, or other wounds easily overlooked or misdiagnosed. Further, veterans should control their health-care benefits and be empowered to seek treatment at both not-for-profit and for-profit facilities. And the federal government must assiduously inspect and maintain facilities and programs to root out waste, fraud, and abuse in order to guarantee that our veterans are treated with the honor, dignity, and care they've so nobly earned.

Second, government must grant tax relief to employers chosen by veterans through a one-time tax credit that he or she can use at any time on any employer to enhance his marketability. Moreover, the government must streamline and expand educational assistance for troops so they may rapidly transition to civilian service to our nation. And the government must punish employers who discriminate against our troops and veterans because of their service to us.

Third, government must ensure that veterans receive the full financial benefits they deserve. That means completely fixing what is known as "concurrent receipt," which allows veterans to receive military retired pay along with disability payment from the Department of Veterans Affairs. And even more important, we must increase our troops' pay—period!

Finally, government must promptly present veterans with their honors and medals, and strengthen its coordination with Veteran Service Organizations.

Truly, these brave men and women joined in the call to defend our country and gave all that they could offer of themselves. We must do the same for them.

Beyond recognizing the debt we owe our military, we must commemorate—and emulate—those who gave their lives for us by pledging to live our lives for each other and for all our fellow human beings suffering in bondage.

Our troops have always embodied our nation's exceptional mission in a world of tyranny and miseries. As Horowitz puts it, "If the United States did not exist, the Communist empire would still be standing, the Taliban would rule Afghanistan, Saddam Hussein would be in power, and the world would be a place of infinitely greater cruelty, injustice, and tragedy than the world that confronts us today."

Throughout the epic sweep of human history's organized nation-states, the United States was, is, and must remain the greatest force for moral good in the world.

Of course, when my friend Miles returned to Karen and their kids after his tour of duty in Iraq, he didn't have to tell them that.

They already knew.

5

Deter the Dragon

"The More Things Change . . ."

Across the political spectrum, politicians deny that the People's Republic of China (PRC) is a strategic threat and rival model of government to America. They even argue that the regime is "not really Communist"—*despite the fact that the regime calls itself Communist.* The Heritage Foundation's John Tkachik has identified this dysfunctional ideology as the "China Fantasy."

The China Fantasy lobby excuses the PRC's ideological mantra that liberty is a threat to Chinese prosperity and security, a claim that is antithetical to Americans' faith that our liberty is the *foundation* of our prosperity and security. While this lobby turns a blind eye to the reality of the Beijing regime, we must frankly acknowledge Communist China's true nature.

In the PRC the Communist Party, not the government,

is the supreme ruler. Though Beijing claims that democracy has increased through a few selected "elections," voters can only choose among eight small, officially registered parties controlled by the Chinese Communist Party. No political opposition groups legally exist; no free and independent labor unions are permitted; and the regime has branded the China Democracy Party as a subversive group. In matters spiritual, the officially atheist regime's State Administration for Religious Affairs, which controls all matters of faith, has persecuted Falun Gong practitioners, outlawed Bibles distributed without state permission, and declared an "official Catholic Church," forcing the true Catholic Church underground and the pope to name "secret cardinals."

The PRC's human rights abuses do not end there. Those resisting the regime are imprisoned in its gulag system, the *Laogai*, where they are exploited as slave laborers and/or executed. Ghoulishly, the regime routinely harvests and sells these victims' organs for transplants or their entire corpses for foreign exhibitions. In a cruel custom, the butchers often charge victims' families for the bullets that killed their loved ones.

The U.S. State Department's 2005 and 2006 Human Rights Reports named Communist China as one of the worst human-rights violators. Amazingly, however, the China Fantasy lobby succeeded in dropping the PRC from the State Department's 2007 list of top ten abusers. In an obtuse statement, Secretary of State Condoleezza Rice— who thought it was America's job to help usher this Communist dictatorship onto the world stage rather than into the dustbin of history—opined, "In the long run, we are confident that citizens who sacrifice for their dignity and their rights will prevail, just as the Havels and the Mandelas did before them. . . . Change will take time, but change will come." Rice did not hazard a guess as to how long these persecuted dissidents, now abandoned by the United States, must wait for their freedom.

Such is the betrayal of liberty caused by the China Fantasy lobby's policy of "unilateral peaceful coexistence." According to these sophisticated elites, the PRC is not Communist but "authoritarian," meaning that it is experiencing economic growth and social change without political reforms. By this definition, Stalin's Russia wasn't Communist and Mussolini's Italy wasn't fascist; they were "authoritarian." Sometimes, too, China Fantasy lobbyists describe Chinese Communists as "nationalists" or "illiberals." Whatever the fashionable term, the China Fantasy lobby's goal is the same: to rebrand a dangerous regime.

Unlike the China Fantasists in the United States, Beijing will candidly state its true ambitions. In 2007, for example, Yang Liwei, the first PRC astronaut in space, boasted that the PRC's space-based Communists would "carry out the regular activities of a Communist Party of China branch in space in the way we do on Earth. Like foreign astronauts having their beliefs, we believe in communism, which is also a spiritual power."

Apparently, for the Communist PRC the sky is not the limit.

The regime possesses more terrestrial aims as well. As Reuters reported on February 28, 2010, a senior officer in the Chinese People's Liberation Army (PLA), Liu Mingfu, published a book in which he boasted, "China's big goal in the 21st century is to become world number one, the top power." The biggest obstacle? The United States. "As long as China seeks to rise to become world number one . . . then even if China is even more capitalist than the U.S., the U.S. will still be determined to contain it." Why? Because, according to Liu, it is a "competition to be the leading country, a conflict over who rises and falls to dominate the world." Thus, "to save itself, to save the world, China must prepare to become the [world's] helmsman." And in his less than humble opinion, Liu advises his fellow Communists that to accomplish this, "We need a military rise as well as an economic rise." This "rise" must occur despite the fact that he shares the conclusion of his fellow author and PLA officer Colonel Dai Xu that with the United States, "China cannot escape the calamity of war, and this calamity may come in the not-too-distant future, at most in 10 to 20 years."

Will the West's China Fantasy awaken to the threat of Beijing's "China Dream"? If not, is there any chance that the West's "sophisticated" lobbying and trade initiatives will bring the Communist regime to its knees before we go broke and they go ballistic?

Monte Hall Maoists

Even if the West didn't, the PRC learned from the Soviet Union's demise. From the 1989 massacre of student protestors in Tiananmen Square to the present, the PRC has sought to avoid the USSR's fate. Consequently, these Monte Hall Maoists have ruthlessly and cunningly cut a deal with the Chinese people: in return for retaining power, the regime would adapt its ideology to the global age and implement a four-pronged strategy to bring prosperity, security, and international supremacy to the "Middle Kingdom."

First, there would be no internal reforms expanding political freedom. The Beijing regime would not repeat the mistake Soviet leader Mikhail Gorbachev made with *Glasnost*, which unleashed democratic forces that destroyed the Soviet Union and incited the crowds in Tiananmen Square. Thus the PRC has an entirely state-controlled media, persecutes religion, cyber-spies on its own citizens, conducts political reeducation in its *Laogai* labor camps, and rigidly adheres to a party line that claims the enemy of prosperity and security is liberty.

Second, the regime had to prevent the West from strangling it economically, as Reagan had done to the Soviets. *Glasnost* overwhelmed the Soviet Union's political structure before the nascent *Perestroika* reforms could save it. So the PRC instituted economic reforms without accompanying political reforms. That way Beijing could ameliorate the material privations of its captive people and preempt massive social unrest from blossoming into a revolution for freedom. Of course, it didn't hurt that the members of the Chinese Communist Party and their relatives would profit from the fruits of the new entrepreneurs' labors.

Third, the PRC promotes a mercantilist, predatory economy. Following the United States' limp response to Tiananmen Square, the Beijing regime was convinced that Americans cared about money, not liberty. The PRC commenced its internal economic reforms and offered American companies and consumers access to cheap Chinese labor and products in return for U.S. dollars. Ignoring this

arrangement's unemployment, trade deficit, and debt ramifications for America, President Clinton and a Republican
Congress granted the PRC the Permanent Normalization
of Trade Relations.

To date, the PRC's strategy has been wildly successful. Although it is a nonmarket nation where the Communist government still dictates five-year plans, in 2003
the PRC overtook America as the world's leading destination for foreign investment. In 2008 it surpassed America
as the world's second-biggest exporter and is closing in on
the number-one exporter, Germany, despite the warning
of the U.S.-China Economic and Security Review Commission (USCC) that "China's control and manipulation
of information make it difficult or impossible for officials
responsible for food and product safety in the United States
and other nations to identify potential safety problems in
Chinese imports on a timely basis and intervene." By 2011,
the PRC is projected to become the world's greatest manufacturing nation.

This mercantilist strategy has allowed the PRC to accumulate an annual trade surplus of more than $250 billion,
control roughly $1.5 trillion of America's national debt,
increase its military capabilities, and expand its access to
raw materials and strategic positions throughout the world.
The USCC's 2009 annual report sums up the situation when
it states that Beijing's "more than $2.27 trillion in foreign
exchange reserves by September 2009 is the world's largest
cache, most of which is in dollar denominated bonds. The
United States today no longer is the world's biggest creditor; it is the world's biggest debtor, with China as the largest overseas holder of U.S. debt instruments."

Fourth, the Communist regime pursued a strategy of unrestricted warfare against its number-one enemy, the country it calls the "Hegemon"—that is, America. The PRC is using every conceivable means to weaken its opponent so that victory is achieved before a bullet is fired. This strategy has a quartet of components: a massive military buildup, cyber warfare, old-school espionage, and the use of commercial and trade practices to infiltrate and/or decimate America's economic capabilities, especially in its high-tech and manufacturing bases. Oh, it also has an elementary operating axiom, which was succinctly articulated by former PRC "president" Jiang Zemin: "Seduce with money; intimidate with force."

Unrestricted Warfare

The intrepid human rights advocate Natan Sharansky, a former Soviet prisoner, warned, "How a government treats its own people cannot be separated from how that government could be expected to treat other countries." Ignoring Sharansky's insight, the China Fantasy lobby dismisses the PRC's unrestricted warfare against America. This weakness emboldens the PRC to expose its aims more brazenly.

Consider this March 28, 2009, article from the Associated Press:

> The only major economy still growing at a fast clip, China is being unusually forthright in challenging the U.S.-led global order. . . . In his second rebuke of U.S. leadership this past week, the central bank gov-

ernor, Zhou Xiaochuan, said China's rapid response to the downturn . . . proved the superiority of its authoritarian, one-party political system.

"Facts speak volumes, and demonstrate that compared with other major economies, the Chinese government has taken prompt, decisive, and effective policy measures, demonstrating its superior system advantage when it comes to making vital policy decisions," Zhou said in remarks posted on the People's Bank of China Web site.

In the single month of March 2008, Communist China (echoing Putin's Russia) called for a new international currency reserve to replace the U.S. dollar, violated international law during a confrontation with a U.S. Navy vessel in the South China Sea, and was revealed by the U.S. Navy to be developing a "carrier killer" missile; meanwhile, its client state, North Korea, fired off a ballistic missile.

Communist China frequently collaborates not only with North Korea but also with Putin's Russia. The Shanghai Cooperation Organization (SCO) is comprised of Communist China, Russia, Kazakhstan, Kyrgyzstan, Tajikistan, and Uzbekistan; it has four observer nations, Mongolia, India, Pakistan, and Iran (which seeks full membership); and it has Sri Lanka and the dictatorship of Belarus as dialogue partners. The SCO is consensus driven, with all decisions made by its Council of Heads of State, which meets annually. But in practice, Communist China and Russia use the SCO to exert and expand their regional influence and hamper American energy supplies. Ultimately, there is a more ominous goal: while the SCO lacks mutual-defense guarantees or a military command, it does hold joint military exercises. Guess who their mock enemy resembles?

In a final memo to his colleagues, former chairman of the House Armed Services Committee Duncan Hunter assessed the status of the PRC's unrestricted warfare:

> China's emergence as a military superpower is being financed by U.S. trade dollars, fueled by the translocation of our industries, guided by technology breakthroughs that our taxpayer-funded laboratories and universities make readily available to any takers, and assisted by the vulnerability of U.S. military technology to a systematic and wide-ranging theft operation.

Not surprisingly, then, the Chinese PLA operates an official cyber warfare division. Its goal is to disrupt all enemy military and civilian communications in a time of war, and to steal military and commercial secrets. The gravest example of the PLA's progress in cyber warfare was the June 2007 infiltration of the U.S. Defense Department's computer networks that forced the system to shut down. Such hostile cyber intrusions continue almost daily against U.S. and Western governmental, military, and economic institutions. According to Lieutenant General Daniel Leaf (U.S. Air Force), deputy commander of the U.S. Pacific Command, the PRC's attacks on American computer systems "would not be consistent" with Beijing's claim to be a peaceful rising power.

As for standard espionage, in 2008 the *Washington Post* reported that the FBI had broken a PRC "sleeper cell" that had been spying in the United States for almost thirty years. U.S. intelligence agencies and Justice Department officials cited in the article said they believed the case was part of a far larger PRC operation. The *Post* reported:

> The case represents only a small facet of an intelligence-gathering operation that has long been in place and is growing in size and sophistication. . . . The Chinese government, in an enterprise that one senior official likened to an "intellectual vacuum cleaner," has deployed a diverse network of professional spies, students, scientists and others to systematically collect U.S. know-how. . . . FBI Director Robert S. Mueller III cited "substantial concern" about aggressive attempts to use students, scientists and "front companies" to acquire military secrets. . . .
>
> "The intelligence services of the People's Republic of China pose a significant threat both to the national security and to the compromise of U.S. critical national assets," said William Carter, an FBI spokesman. . . . While military technology appears to be the top prize, the Chinese effort is also aimed at commercial and industrial technologies, which often are poorly protected, several officials said.

In stealing such technologies, the PLA has established intimate ties with PRC "commercial" ventures. While it is the charge of the Committee on Foreign Investment in the United States (CFIUS) to review and, where necessary, block commercial deals that would endanger American security, stopping PRC and PLA attempts to infiltrate our country has proven a daunting task.

The *Washington Times*'s Bill Gertz reported on one key instance that typifies what CFIUS is up against. In 2007 CFIUS managed to thwart a deal that would have allowed a PRC company "up to its eyeballs with the Chinese military" (according to one official) to buy into an American company that is a world leader in technologies designed to protect secure computer networks from hackers—including technologies extensively used by the U.S. Department of Defense. The PRC firm was set up in 1988 by a former PLA officer to build military communications networks. Former Pentagon cyber-security expert Sami Saydjari said the deal was "really worrisome," while an active Pentagon official judged it as tantamount to "proposing to sell the PLA a key to our front door. This is a very dangerous trend."

We can gauge just how dangerous from the congressional testimony of nuclear-weapons expert Gary Milhollin. Appearing before the House Armed Services Committee on September 19, 2002, Professor Milhollin, director of the Wisconsin Project on Nuclear Arms Control, testified: "Sensitive American exports can wind up threatening our own armed forces. . . . So, when we talk about export controls, we are not just talking about money. We are talking about body bags."

Agreeing with Professor Milhollin, the USCC's 2007 annual report warned that "Chinese espionage activities in the United States are so extensive that they comprise the single greatest risk to the security of American technologies." Communist China wages this "aggressive and large-scale industrial espionage campaign" against American companies located here and in the PRC in order to acquire our technologies "without the necessity of investing time or money to perform research." The report implored Congress to strengthen "military, intelligence, and homeland security programs that monitor and protect critical American computer networks and sensitive information, specifically those tasked with protecting networks from damage caused by cyber attacks."

In 2009 the USCC reasserted its findings:

> The intelligence services of the Chinese government are actively involved in operations directed against the United States and against U.S. interests. China is the most aggressive country conducting espionage against the United States, focusing on obtaining U.S. information and technologies beneficial to China's military modernization and economic development. . . .
>
> The Chinese government has institutionalized many of its capacities for computer network operations within elements of the People's Liberation Army (PLA). The PRC . . . is recruiting skilled cyber operators from information technology firms and computer science programs into the ranks of numerous Information Warfare Militia units.
>
> China's peacetime computer exploitation efforts are primarily focused on intelligence collection against U.S. targets and Chinese dissident groups abroad.
>
> In the early stages of a conflict, the PLA would employ computer network operations against opposition government and military information systems.
>
> Critical infrastructure in the United States is vulnerable to malicious cyber activity. Chinese military

doctrine calls for exploiting these vulnerabilities in the case of a conflict.

In response, the Obama administration has moved oversight of technology transfers back to the Commerce Department and downgraded the PRC as a target for American intelligence gathering. Epitomizing its China Fantasy ideology, the administration's "cyber czar," Howard Schmidt, has publicly stated: "There is no cyber war. I think that is a terrible metaphor and I think that is a terrible concept. There are no winners in that environment." The PRC disagrees.

In a particularly painful passage for working Americans, the USCC's report stressed how small- and medium-sized U.S. manufacturers—representing more than half of all domestic manufacturing jobs—"face the full brunt of China's unfair trade practices, including currency manipulation and illegal subsidies for Chinese exports."

The USCC's report also urged increased U.S. intelligence investigations into whether the PRC was acquiring military technology from research conducted by American firms in China. Other unfair practices include the regime's disregard for intellectual-property rights and the environment.

Ultimately, the PRC can engage in such predatory trade practices to keep its trade relationship with the United States "severely out of balance" because it "maintains a preference for authoritarian controls over its economy"; the Communist regime can keep its "sophisticated weapon platforms . . . coming off production lines at an impressive pace and with impressive quality."

Thus are the PRC's designs on America's technological innovations matched by its efforts to decimate the "Arsenal of Democracy," our manufacturing base. Once again, the Communist regime has learned the lessons of history far better than U.S. policy makers: effective national defense is impossible if America's manufacturing base is eroded. And today, *in a time of war*, our manufacturing base is shrinking.

In response to reality's alarm bell, the China Fantasy lobby hit the snooze button.

A Rain of Riches

Communist China was once teetering on the rim of history's dustbin. But since President Clinton signed the Permanent Normalization of Trade Relations with the PRC on May 24, 2000, the West has unleashed a rain of riches upon the Chinese. Thanks to this "Make Loot, Not War" strategy, the PRC has the world's fastest-growing economy.

Given Western elites' odes to this vanguard of the proletariat's new penchant for riches, one is tempted to assume that these kinder, gentler Chinese neo-Communists are conscientiously using their newfound wealth to advance worthy causes, such as promoting dolphin-free tuna and refurbishing the Clinton Library's "jungle room." But evidently they believe charity begins at home. Communist China's defense spending annually increases by double digits, though its domestic consumer consumption is governmentally repressed. This is not to say that Beijing's priorities are exclusively martial and parochial. Overall, the PRC is spending the boatloads of money we ship it to acquire resources from and to cement its relations with Iran, Cuba, Venezuela, and, yes, Comrade Putin's Russia. The China Fantasy lobby tells us we shouldn't worry and accuses those who do of wanting to start a new Cold War. But shouldn't we be a wee bit concerned that our unilateral peaceful coexistence with the PRC won't lead to mutual peaceful coexistence? For, after all our diplomatic and commercial candies and bouquets sent to court them, the regime is growing more repressive, as an April 2010 *Asia News* story revealed.

In that article, Renée Xia, director of China Human Rights Defenders, cited his organization's 2009 annual report to note that "2009 stands out as a particularly repressive year in terms of the Chinese government's aggressive tactics against human rights activists." Evidently all our Western investment has fueled this growing repression: "The government's growing economic and international power has contributed to a rising confidence and assertiveness among China's leaders, and may have boosted officials' confidence in pressing particularly hard on human rights defenders in the past year."

When not counting our money and cracking down on dissidents in pursuit of his "harmonious society," supreme leader Hu Jintao and his PRC comrades are also

◆ complicit in arming our enemies.
◆ engaging in espionage and cyber warfare against us.
◆ committing predatory trade practices against us.
◆ trying to replace the dollar with the Chinese renminbi as a world reserve currency.

- ◆ abetting genocide in the Sudan.
- ◆ practicing cultural genocide in occupied Tibet.
- ◆ compelling a "one-child policy" that forces abortions amongst its people.
- ◆ denying its people's God-given human rights.
- ◆ violating basic labor rights.
- ◆ buying billion of dollars of oil from state sponsor of terror Iran.

In sum, the China Fantasy lobby unwittingly supports the PRC's assertion that it is a rival model of governance—prosperity and stability without liberty—and the "wave of the future." Unfortunately, the rest of the world is noticing. The USCC's 2009 report observes that in the wake of the 2009 Strategic and Economic Dialogue between the United States and China:

> Many commentators saw the exchange of rebukes on the Chinese side and assurances on the American side as a sign of a power shift between the two countries, in which an assertive China seeks to protect its investment while the United States mutes its criticism because it depends on China's purchases of the Treasuries to finance the economic recovery. And, indeed, during the Strategic and Economic Dialogue, the U.S. side was "quiet on human rights and muted on the [unfair currency valuation issue]."

Unlike the China Fantasy sophisticates, we know how this relationship ends for us, don't we? Time to get the message: rather than becoming our partner, Communist China aims to become a rival model of governance and, ultimately, the globally dominant nation.

To halt this disaster, America and her free allies must curtail the Beijing regime's ambitions and expand liberty to the Chinese people through a strategy of "constructive containment."

Constructive Containment

In defeating the Soviet Union, President Reagan followed two policy dicta: "Peace through strength" and "Trust but verify." We must do the same as we face our global generation's nuclear-armed Communist threat, the PRC.

America needs a twenty-first-century military capable of defeating the terrorist enemy through counterinsurgency and surgical strikes and of simultaneously deterring our nation-state enemies through conventional capabilities. This requires dedicating at least 5 percent of "discretionary" spending to our military.

Meanwhile, the United States must preserve its power to unilaterally deter aggressors and defend itself, which requires the ability to manufacture weapons that make credible the policy of peace through strength. This means that we must stop the predatory trade practices of the PRC and end the outsourcing of our manufacturing base to their shores. If the dismantlement of our Arsenal of Democracy continues, our global generation will witness the hellish spectacle of a president of the United States preemptively appeasing—or even surrendering to—the enemies of freedom.

In addition to enhancing our domestic defense capabilities, we must also build upon our historic and successful alliances through the North Atlantic Treaty Organization (NATO). Given the dangers posed by the proliferation of weapons of mass destruction, America and her NATO allies must install a missile defense shield to deter and defend against the increasing missile capabilities of rogue nations such as Iran and North Korea.

Equally, NATO's mission must be refocused to match the global dangers of our age. Its past mission of securing the liberty of Western Europe and the United States against Soviet aggression must be expanded to defend against all organized threats to liberty. Logically, then, NATO membership must be open to all free nations. Further, NATO must strengthen intelligence and security operations by expanding human intelligence gathering, increasing the accuracy of analysis, intensifying counterintelligence to catch foreign spies, securing and enhancing military and industrial cyber defenses, and toughening rules governing the sale of military weaponry to prevent it from falling into our enemies' hands.

Diplomatically, the United States cannot afford to follow the puerile policy of "peace through speech." Aggressor nations do not measure their "international standing" the same way democracies do. Aggressor nations aim to be feared, not liked. Through intimidation and coercion they seek what they cannot accomplish through cooperation and negotiation—the political subordination of other nations. In pursuing their aims, they anticipate the West's tepid words and don't give a damn. The proper goal of diplomacy, then, is to ensure that aggressor nations are measured by their deeds, not their words, and that such regimes know that the cost of their potential aggression exceeds the prospective rewards of aggression. If this proves insufficient to prevent a rogue regime's aggression, the response—either singular or collective, and including the most prudent measures—must be swift, certain, and disproportionate enough both to stop the aggressor nation's actions and to deter other dangerous regimes.

Finally, America must continue to fulfill her historic duty as a beacon of freedom to and emancipator of oppressed peoples by promoting the moral cause of "security through liberty."

First, regarding the PRC in particular, we must oppose the Communist regime's territorial claims over democratic Taiwan, support the liberation of Tibet and the end of genocide in the Sudan, and reinvigorate our alliances with free Pacific and central Asian nations, especially India.

Second, in response to the economic aspects of the PRC's "unrestricted warfare," we must tie human rights to trade. That is, if other nations are to receive an annual renewal of their trade status, they must honor political and religious freedoms, free and independent labor unions, environmental protections, and import safety. Further, we must insist that before exporting products to America, trade partners implement—and pay for—"reverse inspections" (where items are inspected by the exporting nation) and a transparent recall system. Also, the United States must consistently press our international rights against illegal and unfair trade practices, notably in the areas of intellectual-property rights, counterfeiting, dumping, and currency manipulation. Equally, we must prevent the importation of state socialism to our shores by forbidding so-called Sovereign Wealth Funds from purchasing and controlling American assets and entities. To prevent our technological and other exports from being used against us, CFIUS must emphasize American national security over international commerce. Finally, we must put our fiscal house in order and immediately begin reducing the outstanding U.S. debt held by this Communist regime.

The United States need not act on its own in standing up to the PRC and other aggressor nations. But the United Nations as currently constituted is not the answer. The UN is a global Tammany Hall, lethal to the liberty and dignity of our human family. According to Freedom House, of 192 UN member states, only 89 are "fully free." In other words, a solid majority of member states are repressive regimes. Such regimes, as Claudia Rosett reports, exploit the UN's forum to proffer "evidence of the dignity and respect enjoyed by these governments at the world's leading conclave of nations." No wonder the UN Human Rights Council includes members more suited to a rogues' gallery than a roster of righteous nations.

America's association with this madness exacts a steep price. The United States has been the UN's largest annual contributor since the organization's founding in 1945. American taxpayers annually fork over hundreds of millions of dollars in dues—more than 20 percent of the UN's regular budget—and billions more in total to the UN subsidies. In fact, the UN's top ten financial contributors are all free nations, even though unfree nations are the majority of UN members. The United States and other free nations are being exploited by the UN's corrupt and repressive regimes, and it is high time we stopped paying such a steep premium only to get slapped in the face.

Free nations cannot afford to rely on the UN for even an iota of security. Our survival at stake, all free nations must prudently diminish their participation in a debased UN and unite in the cause of human dignity and liberty. To foster the world's newest births of freedom requires a new international home: the Liberty Alliance.

The Liberty Alliance could be created from the existing Community of Democracies, but it would be a more focused and potent international organization. It would be dedicated to freedom and steeped in the wisdom that liberty's expansion is the best defense against tyranny.

To be a member in the Liberty Alliance, a nation must be free, meeting the alliance's mutually agreed-upon criteria of human and civil rights. Member nations that backslide and diminish their people's liberty beyond the agreed-upon criteria must be demoted to observer status and, when necessary, expelled from the alliance.

Not possessed of a military component, the Liberty Alliance would advance freedom through diplomatic, political, and economic initiatives focused on empowering and emancipating individuals, communities, and emerging democratic governments. The alliance would never dictate abstract, uniform notions of perfect "Western-style democracy" or "democratic capitalism," which are presumptuous and often destabilizing impositions. Instead, it would help peoples trying to seize their freedom and shape their own destinies as they deem fit.

The United States must lead the establishment of the Liberty Alliance; however, the alliance's headquarters should be sited on the free soil once scarred by colonialism, Communism, fascism, world wars, and the Holocaust—Eastern Europe, where liberty's lamp triumphantly pierced these benighted recesses of evil.

In creating the Liberty Alliance, free nations would not exit the UN. The United States and all free nations should remain in the UN to advance or defend liberty by keeping their enemies close. But we must not be so mad as to pay through the nose to get kicked in our assets. No free nation should pay more to the UN than its lowest-paying tyrants, like North Korea and Burma. Free nations' monies and personnel spared from the UN should be dedicated to the Liberty Alliance.

Doubtless, global elitists will decry the Liberty Alliance as undesirable and/or impossible. They are overwrought and best ignored. All free peoples have paid a steep price for liberty; we will not abandon our reasoned faith in a future graced by free nations.

". . . the More They Stay the Same"

It remains the duty and the honor of every child of the American Revolution to stand as one with his fellow human beings abroad who are striving to break the yoke of tyranny. While it is tempting to wish this burden away, liberty-blessed Americans will continue to help haunted, hunted human beings hungering for freedom.

America and the entire Free World are endangered by the PRC and other dangerous regimes. Despite its commercial makeover and the claims of the China Fantasy lobby, the PRC frankly acknowledges its aim to be a rival model of governance to Western democracy. In alleging that liberty is the enemy of stability and prosperity, the PRC shows that Communism remains an intrinsically materialist, nationalist, and evil system of oppression. The truth remains as Pope John Paul II decreed: Communist ideology is a lie antithetical to the human spirit; freedom is a gift from God to the human spirit.

Inspired by this truth, we must end the shortsighted and injurious "China exception," which tells the world that the United States is devoted to the self-evident truth that all human beings are endowed by their Creator with the inalienable rights to life, liberty, and the pursuit of happiness—except in Communist China.

Of course, the China Fantasy lobby opposes any policy of constructive containment. Its illusory policy of unilateral peaceful coexistence is rank appeasement.

In 1937 British appeasers Stanley Baldwin and Neville Chamberlain castigated Conservative members of Parliament—particularly Winston Churchill—for ignoring "the danger of referring directly to Germany at a time when we are trying to get on terms with that country." Fortunately for freedom, Churchill ignored Baldwin and Chamberlain, not the Nazi menace.

Today, while the China Fantasy lobby plays semantic suicide by claiming that the PRC is "not really Communist," we are fortunate that the late patriot Dr. Constantine C. Menges spoke out: "You have to understand a fundamental truth: China is a threat because it is a nuclear-armed communist dictatorship."

6

CHERISH LIFE

The Deconstruction of Independence

Can a nation founded upon self-evident truths survive the cancer of moral relativism?

In surveying our chaotic age, Pope John Paul II confronted moral relativism's danger to America and the world:

> How many winds of doctrine we have known in recent decades, how many ideological currents? . . . We are moving towards a dictatorship of relativism which does not recognize anything as for certain and which has as its highest goal one's own ego and one's own desires.

Moral relativism's rejection of truth propels us toward disunity and servitude. By asserting that imperfect humans are the sole, subjective judges of their own desires and acts, moral relativism encourages immoral behavior, which is not limited to the sphere of personal sin. In a nation without unifying truths to build consensus, there is only propaganda and force to coerce popular obedience to the politically powerful few.

Sheltered in the traditional institutions of faith, family, community, and country, our American community's truths and virtues are incessantly assaulted by moral relativists who deny truth and pervert principles. The Left seeks to indoctrinate and alienate the individual, eradicate all intermediating institutions standing between the individual and the state, and make the state supreme.

This is not idle speculation. It is the avowed strategy of radicals. Consider, for example, the twentieth-century radical thinker Antonio Gramsci. As his biographer Carl Boggs expounds in *Gramsci's Marxism*, Gramsci believed that over time a radical "integrated culture" would first "advance by stages, initially taking the form of skepticism, doubting, and cynicism about prevailing ideas, theories, and values." In the next phase, "Not only must the old meanings and norms of everyday life be destroyed, but new ones must be constructed in their place."

If Gramsci was too subtle, a like-minded observer, Franz Schurmann, honed the point:

Revolutions do not begin with the thunderclap of a seizure of power—that is their culmination. They start with attacks on the moral-political order and the traditional hierarchy of class statuses. They succeed when the power structure, beset by its own irresolvable contradictions, can no longer perform legitimately and effectively. It is often forgotten that the state has often in the past been rescued by the moral-political order and the class hierarchy (authority) that the people still accepted.

Radical ideology's denial of truth and proselytizing of moral relativism is *deliberately designed* to exacerbate the insanity of our chaotic age by denigrating and replacing God, truth, and virtue with atheism, will, and appetite.

American freedom is founded upon the God-given, inviolable sanctity and dignity of the human being, and it is sustained by the voluntary bonds of faith, family, community, and country. We must reject big government's promotion of moral relativism, political correctness, and ideology. To prevent this intended and impending dictatorship of moral relativism, we must cherish, strengthen, and renew faith, family, community, and country, which alone can morally educate the hearts of a free people and sustain American exceptionalism.

Faith

The Declaration of Independence proclaims the self-evident truth that we are endowed by our Creator with the inalienable rights to life, liberty, and the pursuit of happiness. To protect these God-given rights, Americans established a constitutionally limited, free republic in which the people stood supreme against our servant government. But Americans also understood that if our free republic were to endure, it would require self-government. That is, in recognizing the truth of God, we also accepted that, though we cannot be perfect, we must strive to be virtuous. For it remains as President Theodore Roosevelt noted during his chaotic age: "Unless a man is master of his soul, all other kinds of mastery amount to little."

Moral relativism undermines our self-evident truths because it undermines *truth*. The Left's moral relativists aim to convince us that there is no truth and that there is no Creator responsible for endowing us with rights. With no truth and no God, our rights are no longer inalienable; they are *granted* to the people, and able to be governed, by omnipotent government.

Not surprisingly, then, the moral relativists' first target is religion. Father James V. Schall, S.J., explains how the Left's ideology of moral relativism attacks religion and wreaks societal disintegration: "The modern idea that the only truth is the 'truth' we ourselves make is a narrow view that quickly cuts us off from *what is.* . . . No one will seek the highest if he believes that there is no truth, that nothing is his fault, and that government will guarantee his wants."

Standing against this tide of moral relativism are thousands of years of classical Western philosophy. In his *Nicomachean Ethics*, Aristotle made the case: "The origin we begin from is the belief that something is true." From this, Schall examines truth and our need for it: "Truth is of the spirit, the 'conformity of mind and reality.'" Therefore, to attain an order of the soul we must cradle "the liberty of truth that links generations and friends to each other."

What is cannot be measured or discerned in purely scientific terms. Liberty must be linked to deeper truths than mere intelligence or technical exactitude, as Pope John Paul II urged:

> It is of the greatest importance to re-establish the essential connection between life and freedom. . . . There is no true freedom where life is not welcomed and loved; and there is no fullness of life except in freedom. . . . Love, as a sincere gift of self, is what gives the life and freedom of the person their truest meaning.

For moral wisdom to triumph over moral relativism necessitates a reawakening of our moral imagination. In essence and practice, the moral imagination is heartfelt right reason. As Russell Kirk explained, moral imagination is "the power of ethical perception which strides beyond the barriers of private experience and momentary events" and "aspires to the apprehending of right order in the soul and right order in the commonwealth."

Again, this right order of the soul and state does not come from big brother government. Over and over, ideologues have brutally tried and failed to impose their wills upon peoples by denying the existence of God. The secularist Left is trying to do the same today, seeking to turn the powers of the state against institutions of faith. For the Left understands that G. K. Chesterton was right: "The danger of loss of faith in God is not that one will then believe in nothing, but that one will believe in anything."

To stem this descent into nihilism, we must heed Christopher Dawson's advice:

The recovery of moral control and the return to spiritual order have become the indispensable conditions of human survival. But they can be achieved only by a profound change in the spirit of modern civilization. This does not mean a new religion or a new culture but a movement of spiritual reintegration which would restore that vital relation between religion and culture which has existed at every stage and on every level of human development.

Family

After disordering individual souls by attacking faith, moral relativism assaults the primary unit of society—the family.

This assault insidiously begins during a couple's courtship. Romantic courtship starts the journey to a new family. Yet, once more denying the ultimate source of truth and love—God—moral relativism leaves nothing upon which to found a marriage but ephemeral physical desire and gratification. Sadly, the present culture has amplified such barren self-actualization to the point where the leftist-dominated mass culture that spews moral relativism and filth at youth conspires to detour this journey into lust, loss, and loneliness. Young lovers are seduced into trading romance for "relationships."

Where truth is subjectively defined, individuals are atomized. Only where physical attraction and/or relative truths overlap between individuals is a bond formed, and that bond is ephemeral, because attractions ebb and values change. Atomized suitors are reduced to trying to achieve the unobtainable: managing an unsustainable relationship into a perfect and permanent equilibrium of mutual bliss. In a dictatorship of relativism, where there is no truth except scientific equations, romance is dead. In such an affair of the heartless, two unique lovers' attempts to manage a blossoming romance into a static relationship ends but in regret and recriminations.

Nevertheless, the human heart has its own immutable truths. Each person is a unique, spiritual being possessed of unfathomable depths of emotion and, yes, unpredictability. In their hearts, the young—the romantics of every era—know this. They intuit the thrilling mystery of loving and the exquisite misery of losing a lover who is unique in all eternity. Yes, they know that love—beautiful, unfathomable, eternal, and true—exists. Thus, there is hope.

Unlike moral relativism, which excuses the differences (and everything else) between people as equally meaningless, true love celebrates and bridges these differences. Uniting our frail, unique natures, romance overcomes courtship's complications and deepens love's ecstasy. We are liberated to truly love another with passionate, honest, eternal intensity that transcends even the most mundane moments of our mortal existence.

Further, rapturously loving a person known to be equally unique, one will make self-sacrifices to preserve the romance and all it portends for true happiness. Throughout human history wise minds have advised that there is more to life than hunting for sex without love and consequence. There is love at first sight. There is *the one.*

Today's youth are at heart no different from previous generations that sought love, not equilibrium. This fact portends that they will discard "relationships" for romance. In such a renewed society, sex as exercise becomes inconceivable; divorce becomes dreaded; the foundation of the family becomes more secure; love reigns and life blossoms. Or will it? For moral relativism also assaults the act of procreation.

In another day, people used a phrase to express where a human being was most secure: "You are as safe as in your mother's womb." Today, one no longer hears this phrase.

Our culture coarsened on January 22, 1973, when seven members of the United States Supreme Court willfully and without legal precedent created a constitutional right to abortion. By denying an unborn child's God-given right to life, the *Roe v. Wade* ruling ended the legal protections of unborn children and, unconscionably, their lives. Often neglected, however, is that *Roe v. Wade* equally denigrated the sanctity of human life for all Americans, weakened our democratic institutions, and hastened the decay in America's cherished realms of faith, family, and community.

Roe v. Wade empowered government to determine arbitrarily which innocent human lives deserved protection. The decision ushered in other life-denying and destroying practices—such as assisted suicide—which are premised on the assertion that innocent life is conditional and subject to government.

Moreover, by seizing the contentious abortion issue from the hands of the voters, the Supreme Court—deliberately designed as the least publicly accountable branch of American government—disenfranchised the American people from deciding the issue among themselves through democratic processes and institutions. In fact, by 1973 the abortion issue was being debated and decided by the sovereign American people in states throughout our nation. Some states' citizens liberalized abortion laws; some states' citizens defended the unborn. But most, if not all, Americans were engaged in the issue and pursuing its resolution through civic participation. By arbitrarily deciding the outcome in *Roe v. Wade*, the Supreme Court failed to settle the issue in the public's mind, because the public itself had not settled the issue through the democratic process. As a result of such judicial overreach, voters can no longer be certain that their civic participation will settle contentious issues; many now figure that they shouldn't even bother.

In heralding a coarsened culture accepting of legalized abortion, *Roe v. Wade* eroded America's institutions of faith, family, and community. People of faith cannot fathom how our nation—built upon the self-evident truth that all human beings are endowed by their Creator with inalienable rights—can permit an unborn child to be sacrificed on the altar of adults' "self-actualization." Families, whose most moral and noble duties are to protect and to raise their children, are weakened when the lives of any children—including the unborn—are conditioned upon the feelings of others.

It is as Mother Teresa wrote: "Human rights are not a privilege conferred by government. They are every human being's entitlement by virtue of his humanity. The right to life does not depend, and must not be declared to be contingent, on the pleasure of anyone else, not even a parent or a sovereign." In the wake of the debasement of faith and family, our entire community teeters toward the precipice of moral chaos.

Appropriately, Mother Teresa also stressed what "pro-choice" supporters deliberately ignore—the damaging consequences of abortion upon all women:

> America needs no words from me to see how your decision in *Roe v. Wade* has deformed a great nation. The so-called right to abortion has pitted mothers against their children and women against men. It has sown violence and discord at the heart of the most intimate human relationships. It has aggravated the derogation of the father's role in an increasingly fatherless society. It has portrayed the greatest of gifts—a child—as a competitor, an intrusion, and an inconvenience. It has nominally accorded mothers unfettered dominion over the independent lives of their physically dependent sons and daughters.
>
> And, in granting this unconscionable power, it has exposed many women to unjust and selfish demands from their husbands or other sexual partners.

"Any country that accepts abortion," Mother Teresa added, "is not teaching its people to love, but to use any violence to get what it wants." Thus women now must confront a diabolical choice: "It is a poverty to decide that a child must die so that you may live as you wish."

Tragically, in the years since *Roe v. Wade*, our society has ignored Pope John Paul II's appeal to our moral sensibilities: "America, you are beautiful and blessed in so many ways. . . . The ultimate test of your greatness is the way you treat every human being, especially the weakest and most defenseless. If you want equal justice for all and true freedom and lasting peace, then America, defend life."

If we do not defend life, we will all continue to live amidst a degraded American culture and a more brutal world where "we are all as unsafe as in our mother's womb." Moral relativism seeks to make us equally unsafe in our families. Edmund Burke famously spoke of the family as the first of society's "little platoons." It is, according to Burke, "the first link in the series by which we proceed towards a love to our country, and to mankind." In other words, the family is the paramount mediating institution standing between the individual and the state. To those who want state control of society, the family represents a threat. Parents who impart their moral teachings to their children, for example, block state indoctrination. As a result, the Left has long sought to weaken the parent-child relationship in order to strengthen the state. In his classic work *The Quest for Community*, sociologist Robert Nisbet described the results of such interventions: "The alleged disorganization of the modern family is, in fact, simply an erosion of its natural authority, the consequence, in considerable part, of the absorption of its functions by other bodies, chiefly the state."

In the mother of all statist attempts to usurp parental rights, the global Left is pushing the United Nations' Convention on the Rights of the Child (CRC). On February 16, 1995, Madeleine Albright, then the U.S. ambassador to the United Nations, signed the CRC on behalf of the United States. Although then–first lady and current secretary of state Hillary Clinton proclaimed the signing of the treaty a great victory, Presidents Bill Clinton and George W. Bush never sent the treaty to the Senate for ratification. Pray no American president ever does. The Left wants the U.S. Senate to ratify the CRC so parental rights are severed and America's children are reared by an international gaggle of lunatics—notably the UN's Committee on the Rights of the Child, which under the CRC you don't get to vote out of office.

The CRC is predicated on two core conceits: that the state knows better than parents how to raise their child, and that the child knows better than parents how to raise him- or herself.

The first conceit is evident in CRC Article 3(1), which provides: "In all actions concerning children, whether undertaken by public or private social welfare institutions, courts of law, administrative authorities or legislative bodies, the best interests of the child shall be a primary consideration."

Geraldine Van Bueren, a professor of human rights law at the University of London who helped draft the CRC, bluntly explains this provision's purpose: "Unlike earlier treaties, the Convention on the Rights of the Child does not include a provision providing for parents to have their children educated in conformity with their parents' beliefs."

With whose beliefs, then, will the child have to conform? A UN commission ruled by people like Van Bueren. Article 12(1) provides: "States Parties shall assure to the child who is capable of forming his or her own views the right to express those views freely in all matters affecting the child, the views of the child being given due weight in accordance with the age and maturity of the child."

Again, Van Bueren states the objective more frankly:

> The child's right to freedom of expression and the
> right of the parents to initially give direction and
> later only guidance, strengthens the argument that
> children are entitled to participate in decisions so that
> their education conforms to their own convictions.

Under the guise of giving the child a "voice," it is the
state that will make the ultimate determination of what is
in the child's best interest.

This is a patently socialist goal. Michael P. Farris, the
chairman of the Home School Legal Defense Association,
has written an in-depth study of the CRC entitled *Nannies
in Blue Berets*. In it he identifies the CRC's ultimate ambi-
tion when he describes the "human rights theory" that
is at the heart of the CRC. Farris writes, "The traditional
American theory of rights—as represented by documents
like our Bill of Rights—are guarantees of liberty that act
as limitations on the power of government." Human rights
theory, he adds, "embraces most of these kinds of rights
but contains an entirely different sector of rights as well. In
short, human rights theory contains the right to complete
care from a socialistic state—not just for children, but for
all persons."

Van Bueren, seemingly bent upon proving that it takes
a global village idiot to raze a family, admits as much when
she describes the "change" that CRC aims to accomplish:

> International human rights law is a peaceful but pow-
> erful instrument of change. In essence, human rights
> is about peacefully redistributing unequal power. . . .
> Political philosophies that undermine social welfare

on the basis of privacy are not acceptable. . . . The CRC provides an ideology for state intervention.

"An ideology for state intervention." Here we see another manifestation of the urge to terminate parental rights. This has been an objective of ideologues since the time of Rousseau, whose idyllic state of nature included no parents, only procreators. Van Bueren goes further when she writes that international law is "establishing boundaries within which states are under a duty to ensure that parental power is properly exercised and within limits. . . . The international protection of children's civil rights now touches the core of family life."

And here you had no idea that such rude leftist guests had infested your home. Well, here are some of the housewarming gifts their CRC has in store for you.

Americans' sovereignty would be lost along with parental rights. The CRC would supersede nearly every American statute regarding children and families. In interpreting this new treaty's impact on Americans, the least accountable branch of our government—the federal courts—would be empowered to determine and/or directly enforce the CRC's "self-executing" provisions. Further, Congress would be empowered—even required—to pass legislation specifically to comply with the CRC's provisions. As Farris warns, "This would constitute the most massive shift of power from the states to the federal government in American history."

If congressional bums vitiating parental rights weren't enough, the UN bums on the CRC's committee—eighteen foreign "experts" pontificating from Geneva—would have the power to issue official interpretations of the treaty with binding weight in American courts and legislatures. Effectively, this means that a stranger could tell an American parent how to raise his or her child.

The jobs of American parents would be outsourced, and state child rearing would be the norm, as Farris states:

> Children would have the ability to choose their own religion while parents would only have the authority to give their children advice about religion. The best interest of the child principle would give the government the ability to override every decision made by every parent if a government worker disagreed with the parent's decision. A child's "right to be heard" would allow him (or her) to seek governmental review of every parental decision with which the child disagreed. . . . Children would acquire a legally enforceable right to leisure. Christian schools that refuse to teach "alternative worldviews" and teach that Christianity is the only true religion [would] "fly in the face of article 29" of the treaty. Allowing parents to opt their children out of sex education has been held to be out of compliance with the CRC. Children would have the right to reproductive health information and services, including abortions, without parental consent.

Farris sums up the impact CRC would have on American parents and children if the U.S. Senate ratified it:

> By virtue of the ratification of this treaty, Congress would not only acquire the duty to implement the

treaty, Congress would also acquire the jurisdiction necessary to directly legislate on education, health care, and regulation of family life. . . . The CRC is a human rights treaty which mandates a socialistic duty of the government to furnish a child's needs in economic, social, and cultural areas.

Thus, despite the overwhelming evidence of the need for loving, united families, the Left's implacable assault on them continues apace. And it is working, as Joseph Pearce relates in the book *Small Is Still Beautiful: Economics as If Families Mattered*:

In the past thirty years we have also seen a concerted attack on the family itself and on the traditional understanding of marriage. . . . Families form the smallest and most beautiful part of any healthy society. . . . They are, in fact, the building blocks upon which all healthy societies are erected. Take away the family from the heart of society and you are left with a heartless hedonism. And since hedonism is selfishness without limits, it is the very antithesis of the self-limitation necessary for the restoration of economic and political sanity.

To fend off the Left's assault, a just government will shelter and support the family, not usurp its rights and role, and it will leave children's spiritual, moral, and educational development in the surest hands for their fulfillment—parents, not the government. As Robert Nisbet wrote:

It is the family, not the individual, that is the real molecule of society, the key link of the social chain of being. . . . The great contributions of kinship to society are, on the one hand, the sense of membership in and continuity of the social order, generation after generation; and, on the other, the spur to individual achievement, in all areas, that the intimacy of the family alone seems able to effect.

Truly, then, the family's intimacy must be inviolable.

Community

In 1971 the Left issued its declaration of war against American community. The author was Saul Alinsky, a Chicago radical who with an evil irony dubbed himself a "community organizer." Alinsky's screed was titled *Rules for Radicals: A Pragmatic Primer for Realistic Radicals.*
Alinsky kicks off the book with this dedication:

From all our legends, mythology, and history (and who is to know where mythology leaves off and history begins—or which is which), the first radical known to man who rebelled against the establishment and did it so effectively that he at least won his own kingdom—Lucifer.

Amazingly, *Rules for Radicals* goes downhill from there. In the prologue, Alinsky announces that he has come to claim "those young radicals who are committed to the fight, committed to life." Sounding more like he should be committed *for* life, he lays out a plan to subvert our free republic's institutions from within and to impose his radical revolution from above:

> Any revolutionary change must be preceded by a passive, affirmative, non-challenging attitude toward change among the mass of our people. They must feel so frustrated, so defeated, so lost, so futureless in the prevailing system that they are willing to let go of the past and change the future. This acceptance is the reformation essential to any revolution. To bring on this reformation requires that the organizer work inside the system.

As for his rules to accomplish this "revolutionary change," it doesn't take a Harvard Law School graduate to understand Alinsky's "community organizing" tactics. For starters, Alinsky revels in moral relativism: "That perennial question, 'Does the end justify the means?' is meaningless as it stands: the real and only question regarding the ethics of means and ends is, and always has been, 'Does this particular end justify this particular means?'" So much for universal truths and traditional morality.

Alinsky next argues that acts be viewed through an amoral prism of pragmatism: "The ethics of means and ends is that generally success or failure is a mighty determinant of ethics." Succinctly, it's moral if it works.

Of course, this means that any act, including deceit, is acceptable if it attains the desired end. As Alinsky puts it, "You do what you can with what you have and clothe it with moral garments." And if this subterfuge is insufficient, one can always disguise one's true ends: "Goals must be phrased in general terms like 'Liberty, Equality, Fraternity,' 'Of the Common Welfare,' 'Pursuit of Happiness,' or 'Bread and Peace.'"

Damned by his own words (and his plagiarism of Lenin), the devious relativist Alinsky is not engaged in "community organizing" to empower people or inspire them to control their own lives, since that would only strengthen community and society's other intermediating institutions. Quite the opposite, Alinsky's aim is community *disorganizing*—dispiriting and directing the increasingly alienated to demand a highly centralized federal government, so that his radical ilk can dictate socialist revolution from Washington.

Alinsky died just a year after *Rules for Radicals* was published, but his message has been heard and followed by a whole lot of lefties, including a former campus radical who is now secretary of state and an erstwhile community organizer who is now president of the United States. They have yet to publicly reject Alinsky's goal of "working within the system" to subsume the powers of citizens and local communities under the "national community" of an increasingly centralized and omnipotent federal government.

In contrast to the morally repugnant nihilist Alinsky and his radical "national community," the champion of true community is the conservative Robert Nisbet. Nisbet took the myth of "national community" head-on: "It is the image of community contained in the promise of the absolute, communal State that seems to have the greatest evocative power." The state itself promotes this false image:

The greatest single influence upon social organization in the modern West has been the developing concentration and power of the sovereign political State. To regard the State as simply a legal relationship, as a mere superstructure of power, is profoundly delusive. The real significance of the modern State is inseparable from its successive penetrations of man's economic, religious, kinship, and legal allegiances, and its revolutionary dislocations of established centers of function and authority.

Unlike the national state, which is contrived and, often, coerced into existence, local community is organic. It grows from what Nisbet identified as our "social impulse" to "form associations," an impulse "that is so fundamental to freedom in any of its significant forms." A community may be entirely or partially composed of differing institutions, including "family, village, parish, town, voluntary association, and class," but it cannot include "the political state."

Of paramount importance is the community's function—its existential purpose, because "nothing is so likely in the long run to lead to the decay of community than the disappearance of the function that established it in the first place." Instinctively sensing a rival to power, the national state greedily usurps a community's functions to expand its control over individuals. This led Nisbet to declare that "the sole object of the conservative tradition is the protection of the social order and its constitutive groups from the enveloping bureaucracy of the national state."

How can our conservative tradition defend our cherished way of life and its community institutions against the national state? Nisbet proposed a new "form of laissez-faire that has for its object, not the abstract individual, whether economic or political man, but rather the social group or association." In essence, Nisbet believed that conservatives should fight against the state's encroachments on local communities by ensuring that these organic, localized institutions have the space to grow.

This does not mean that individuality must be constricted. Quite the contrary:

> The liberal values of autonomy and freedom of personal choice are indispensable to a genuinely free society, but we shall achieve and maintain these by vesting them in the conditions in which liberal democracy will thrive—diversity of culture, plurality of association, and the division of authority.

In implementing a conservative defense of community that allows voluntary associations and individuality to flourish, we must reassert federalism. To respect the states' sovereign powers is to preserve the first lines of defense against an omnipotent federal government.

Equally, community organizations must be protected from both governmental and nongovernmental discrimination. We cannot allow true community to disappear in the name of a mythical "national community"; we must ensure that organic, localized communities serve as an effective guard against an unlimited federal government.

Country

In the Age of Globalization, the Left is not content to impose a "national community" upon our free people; it seeks to impose a "global community" upon our free republic.

Taking Alinsky's radical playbook global, the Left is engaged in national disorganizing. Specifically, the Left aims to end our patriotic reverence for American exceptionalism and turn us into morally relative, secular cosmopolitans who reject God and country in favor of global governance.

In his book *The Cube and the Cathedral*, George Weigel discerned that Europe's cultural and civilizational malaise was caused by the triumph of atheistic humanism's "freedom of indifference" over a faith-based "freedom for excellence."

Europeans misunderstood their own twentieth-century history, concluding that the intractability of obsessively held "truths" had caused two world wars, the Holocaust, and other horrors. They were thus enticed by moral relativism's purported ability to end conflicts by preemptively denying that truth existed—especially the truth of God's existence. In doing so, Europe sank into the abyss of atheistic humanism, which, though professing an abiding concern for human rights, actually masks the inhumane consequences of basing individuals' lives, dignity, and rights upon the will and whims of despots or the mob.

More sage observers knew that it was not God, faith, and truth that caused Europe's twentieth-century depravities. Writing about 1914 and the onset of World War I,

Aleksandr Solzhenitsyn proclaimed that it was precisely the opposite:

> The only possible explanation for [World War I] is a mental eclipse among the leaders of Europe due to their lost awareness of a Supreme Power above them. ... Only the loss of that higher intuition which comes from God could have allowed the West to accept calmly, after World War I, the protracted agony of Russia as she was being torn apart by a band of cannibals. .... The West did not perceive that this was in fact the beginning of a lengthy process that spells disaster for the whole world.

No good government denies God's presence; yet, in Europe, this damning rejection of God continues into the present. The verdict on post-Christian Europe was read by Christopher Dawson: "A secular society that has no end beyond its own satisfaction is a monstrosity—a cancerous growth which will ultimately destroy itself."

The question is whether the Left will be able to induce Americans to follow suit.

The Left incessantly "blames America first," tries to eradicate our patriotic symbols and traditions, and denies the historical reality of America's accomplishments—be it refusing to recite the Pledge of Allegiance, burning our flag, or apologizing for America's enemies (or for America itself). Such efforts assail American exceptionalism and attempt to undercut the United States as the world's only superpower. Seeing America—not Communist China, or Iran, or terrorist organizations—as the world's greatest threat to peace, the Left wants to hand America's sovereignty to international organizations such as the United Nations.

David Willetts, a member of the British Parliament, identifies the damage wrought by attempts to remake nations based on "abstract principles and textbook theories." These ideologues "misunderstand globalization," Willetts says:

> They think "globalization" means that we all get more like each other. They believe that what they have to do as reforming politicians in Britain is to give this historical and economic process a push by legislating to change our constitution or our economic structures so they look more like everyone else's, particularly more like those of the continent of Europe. It is the classic fallacy of the progressive.

But Willetts rightly explains that there can be another future, both for Europe and for the United States: "Conservatives celebrate what is distinctive about their own country. Whereas left-wing rationalists are the same the world over, each nation has its own form of conservatism. Each nation's conservatism celebrates what is distinctive. And globalization does not threaten this: globalization rewards it." Globalization rewards nations for doing what they distinctively do best.

As ours is an exceptional nation, what awaits us?

America's future does not lie in becoming a secular, cosmopolitan, socialist backwater. Our America is beautiful. She does not exist to emulate others; she exists to inspire the world. Her people will keep her that way. There is just one goal Americans seek: to peacefully live in a world of free peoples. For this, God (if not the global Left) will reward us.

Destiny

From the first salvo of their modern war against our enduring realms of faith, family, community, and country, the Left's moral relativists have been open about their strategy and aims. Antonio Gramsci, as Carl Boggs observed, looked to subvert "the institutions and values of bourgeois society by attacking their manifestations in all aspects of everyday life." Such attacks on a people's cherished way of life were central to "the overall revolutionary strategy that . . . comprehends socialist transformation as a process emerging out of grass-roots democratic structures that give shape to the party and prepare the ground for dismantling the old state apparatus while creating an entirely different kind of political order in its place."

Left-wing theoretician Wilhelm Reich further distilled this change fools can believe in: "A global economic and political policy, if it means to create and secure international socialism, must find a point of contact with the trivial, banal, primitive, simple every-day life, with the desires of the broadest masses."

The American Left has followed this strategy, declaring open war on the culture of American civilization. Americans should never wonder why a formerly conservative foundation has started funding leftist front groups; why a formerly nonpartisan organization has suddenly advocated leftist causes; why a faith-based community organization has been demonized and attacked by a leftist-dominated city council; or why a Miss USA contestant is asked her position on same-sex marriage by a leftist on the judges' panel.

To defend American civilization from these unbalanced ideologues requires vigilance, principled opposition, and fidelity to the truth that politics is but a thin thread in life's rich tapestry.

To renew American civilization will require more. We must serve God and truth, order the soul, and govern ourselves. As Russell Kirk warned:

> A man without principles is an unprincipled man. A nation without principles is an uncivilized nation. If a people forget their principles, they relapse into barbarism and savagery. If a people reject sound principles for false principles, they become a nation of fanatics.

Or victims.

Americans are neither fanatics nor victims. Americans are honest, reverent, decent souls who will forever cherish God, truth, life, and their virtuous allegiance to faith, family, community, and country. We *will* defeat the forces of moral relativism. Through our truths we will transcend this chaotic age, renew our American civilization, and realize God's promise unto Daniel: "But the wise will shine brightly, like the splendor of the firmament; and those who lead the many to justice shall be as the stars forever."

Through God's grace, may we all shine on in our beacon of liberty.

7

OUR BLESSED SANCTUARY
OF LIBERTY

America's Salvation

We the people know that America remains "the last best
hope of earth"—a unique beacon of hope and freedom to
the world's oppressed. This blessing and duty is why we
Americans are at our best when challenged. It is why, as
President Abraham Lincoln affirmed on the eve of the
Civil War, America's salvation remains her free people:
"Why should there not be a patient confidence in the ultimate justice of the people? Is there any better or equal hope
in the world?"

There is not, President Theodore Roosevelt answered
during the tumultuous Age of Industrialization:

> We believe in all our hearts in democracy; in the
> capacity of the people to govern themselves; and we
> are bound to succeed, for our success means not only

our own triumph, but the triumph of the cause of the rights of the people throughout the world, and the uplifting of the banner of hope for all the nations of mankind.

There is not, President Ronald Reagan answered during the depths of recession and at the height of Communist expansion:

We are too great a nation to limit ourselves to small dreams. We are not, as some would have us believe, doomed to an inevitable decline. I do not believe in a fate that will fall on us no matter what we do. I do believe in a fate that will fall on us if we do nothing. So, with all the creative energy at our command, let us begin an era of national renewal. Let us renew our determination, our courage, and our strength. And let us renew our faith and our hope. We have every right to dream heroic dreams.

Now *we* must answer Lincoln's question.

Seizing Freedom

In homes, farms, mills, and malls across America, citizens are asking: "What can we do?"

We know that our revolutionary experiment in liberty has created the freest, strongest, and wealthiest nation in the world, and nurtured the expansion of freedom around the world. Still, concerned about the course of our country in these challenging times, we are determined to ensure that our freedom, prosperity, and security endure.

Fortunately, today we can do more for America and one another than any generation in history. Matching entrepreneurial idealism with global technology, in a keystroke we can communicate with Congress, study pending legislation, and discuss issues with citizens across America. These technologies also provide us more time and opportunities to perform the indispensable acts of virtuous citizenship— voting; writing e-mails or snail mail; making phone calls; volunteering with church, civic, and political organizations; supporting or running for elective offices; tutoring students; mentoring troubled youth; donating to charitable organizations; and, yes, attending religious services. As entrepreneurial idealists we can support our enduring institutions of faith, family, community, and country.

Our service to America must be as boundless as our moral imagination and devotion to freedom. Sorely challenged in this chaotic age, we must affirm our faith in ourselves as Americans, expand liberty and self-government, and bequeath the greatest nation on earth to our children.

Will we?

Writing at the close of the twentieth century, Russell Kirk wondered:

> Is the course of nations inevitable? Is there some fixed destiny for great states? . . . At the very moment when some states "seemed plunged in unfathomable abysses of disgrace and disaster," Burke wrote in his *First Letter on a Regicide Peace*, "they have suddenly emerged. They have begun a new course, and opened a new

reckoning; and even in the depths of their calamity, and on the very ruins of their country, have laid the foundations of a towering and durable greatness."

Our ideological Global Age has dealt roughly with our blessed sanctuary of liberty. Lady Liberty's loyal and loving citizenry endures a quartet of transformational challenges: a global recession's economic, political, and social disorders; a War for Freedom against terrorists' *kufar* fascism; the strategic threat and rival model of governance posed by Communist China; and moral relativism's assault upon our self-evident truths.

For some, the strain is too great. They seek the false calm of indifference and defeat. It is an ignoble course they choose, one that will garner little but Wordsworth's epitaph for his troubled epoch:

> The world is too much with us; late and soon,
> Getting and spending, we lay waste our powers;
> Little we see in Nature that is ours;
> We have given our hearts away, a sordid boon!

As the heirs of the American Revolution, we have inherited its triumphs, heroic dreams, and enduring truths. The core of our inheritance is that our liberty is from God, not the government. This is the foundation for the four other truths of American civilization: our sovereignty is in our souls, not the soil; our security is through strength, not surrender; our prosperity is from the private sector, not the public sector; and our truths are self-evident, not relative. Bound by and abiding these American truths, our global generation cradles the hope of humanity. We carry the moral duty to seize freedom and renew American civilization in this age of hope and peril.

This is not a call to a new revolution. It is a call to renew the American Revolution.

To bring order, justice, and freedom, we must calm our nation's economic, political, and social upheavals; grasp our unprecedented opportunities during globalization; defend our liberty and extend it to human beings still yearning to breathe free; and affirm truth in the face of dehumanizing ideology. Only then will we live more freely, securely, and prosperously. Only then will we honor our inherited legacy and ensure that it is bequeathed to our children.

Yes, equally challenged Athens failed, so weighing upon us is a question Kirk asked: "Is it conceivable that American civilization, and in general what we call 'Western civilization,' may recover from the Time of Troubles that commenced in 1914 . . . and in the twenty-first century enter upon an Augustan age of peace and restored order?"

Edmund Burke showed us the way: "Freedom and not servitude is the cure of anarchy; as religion, and not atheism, is the true remedy for superstition." This is the freedom we must seize—the freedom that in the darkest moments of oppression and revolution inspired Abigail Adams to declare:

> These are the times in which a genius would wish to live. It is not in the still calm of life, or the repose of a pacific station, that great characters are formed. . . .

> The habits of a vigorous mind are formed in contending with difficulties. . . . Great necessities call out great virtues. When a mind is raised and animated by scenes that engage the heart, then those qualities, which would otherwise lay dormant, wake into life and form the character of the hero and the statesman.

Heeding her call, we will affirm American truths to renew our nation in this chaotic age. We will fight to ensure that our blessed sanctuary of liberty remains inspired and guided by the virtuous genius of her free people—and eternally blessed by the unfathomable grace of God.

We will seize freedom!

We will be freedom!

For while Russell Kirk wondered about America's twenty-first-century future, he knew that the answer lived in Americans' free souls: "The enlightened conservative does not believe that the end or aim of life is competition; or success; or enjoyment; or longevity; or power; or possessions. He believes, instead, that the object of life is Love."

Loving her, we realize that America is not an economy or a bureaucracy—America is a country. We will ensure that she remains a blessed land of liberty, inspired and guided by the virtuous genius of her free people, and eternally blessed by the unfathomable grace of God.

We are duty bound to heed freedom's summons amid our struggles. And we shall do so with the virtuous courage expressed by the poet Rupert Brooke:

Now, God be thanked

Who has matched us with His hour,

And caught our youth,
And wakened us from sleeping.

Wide awake in this Global Age, we the people will transcend our great challenges and seize this moment to lead America's newest birth of freedom.

Appendix

Conservatism 101

Bone Up!

Welcome to the study of conservatism!

You could not have chosen a more propitious time. The Left, having jumped headlong into radicalism and statism, has intensified the chaos spawned by our four great challenges. Conservatism, the negation of ideology, is precisely what is needed to overcome this crisis.

Only through conservatism can we preserve our best traditions and bring gradual, constructive change, not the radical, destructive change that has characterized the recent past. Such change must be based on principles of empathy, equity, and morality, because in governance Americans rightly demand sanity and disdain ideology.

The Left failed to recognize this crucial point, deluded into believing that its own rhetoric, combined with the GOP's failures, had realigned America into a leftist nation.

As soon as it seized power, the Left embarked on its radical agenda. Predictably, this produced a wave of voter revulsion in a country that remains center-right.

But conservatives cannot become overconfident, lest they repeat the same mistakes that sabotaged the Republicans' "permanent majority." The biggest mistake would be to succumb again to the temptations of ideology.

And make no mistake, many self-proclaimed "conservatives" are ideological tools. To cure them and inoculate others, we must rid their brains of hoary ideologies while soothingly imparting the enduring principles of conservatism.

To find out where you stand, take the following two quizzes. The first measures your understanding of philosophical conservatism; the second, whether you are culturally attuned to the times. If you don't pass both tests, you are a nut and/or a stiff and decidedly not a cultural conservative.

Be advised that these are old-school tests. There are right and wrong answers; there are no bonus points for self-esteem; and you can fail miserably.

Good luck, tiger.

Test 1: The Philosophical Conservatism Quiz

Part I: Conservatism and American Civilization
[Multiple Choice]

Select the best answer from among the following:

1. Conservatives believe the three enduring pillars of
American civilization are:
   a. Order, justice, and freedom
   b. The Canadian power-rock trio Rush
   c. Moe, Larry, and Curly
   d. "Who knows? Who cares? Why bother?"

2. Order without liberty is:
   a. Tyranny
   b. No fun
   c. Bogus
   d. Near

3. Liberty without order is:
   a. Anarchy
   b. Fun
   c. Awesome
   d. Near

4. The competing claims of order and liberty are reconciled by:
   a. Justice
   b. Their marriage counselor
   c. Judge Judy
   d. Jack Daniels

Part II: The Central Tenets of Conservatism [True or False]

As expressed by intellectuals ranging from Edmund Burke to Russell Kirk, conservatism's central tenets hold that:

5. "Men and women are transcendent children of God endowed by their Creator with inalienable rights." *True / False*

6. "Government was instituted to defend citizens' inalienable rights and facilitate citizens' pursuit of the good and of true happiness." *True / False*

7. "Over the generations, Divine Providence has established and revealed through tradition, prescriptive rights, and custom within communities how order, justice, and freedom—each essential, coequal, and mutually reinforcing—are best

arranged and nurtured for humanity to pursue the good and true happiness." *True / False*

8. "Human happiness is endangered by every political ideology, for each is premised upon abstract ideas; each claims a superior insight into human nature not revealed through historical experience; each proffers a secular Utopia unobtainable by an imperfect humanity; and each demands an omnipotent, centralized government to forcefully impose its vision upon an 'unenlightened' and unwilling population." *True / False*

9. "Because both permanence and change are necessary within a vital society, the challenge of today is creative preservation." *True / False*

10. "Politics is part of life." *True / False*

Part III: The Central Tenets of Radicalism
[True or False]

As expressed by lefties ranging from Robespierre to a Regressive blogger named "Mr. Wiggles," radicalism's central tenets hold that:

11. "God is dead." *True / False*

12. "The life of man is solitary, poor, nasty, brutish, and short." *True / False*

13. "Bigger government is progress." *True / False*

14. "All change is good." *True / False*

15. "Politics is life." *True / False*

16. "This is the dawning of the Age of Aquarius." *True / False*

Part IV: Conservatism's Enduring Ideals
[Fill in the Blank]

As Russell Kirk outlined in *The Politics of Prudence*, who believes the following, a conservative or an ideological stiff?

17. _____ believes that there exists an enduring moral order.

18. _____ adheres to custom, convention, and continuity.

19. _____ believes in what may be called the principle of prescription—that is, of things established by immemorial usage.

20. _____ is guided by the principle of prudence.

21. _____ pays attention to the principle of variety.

22. _____ is chastened by the principle of imperfectability.

23. _____ is persuaded that freedom and property are entwined.

24. _____ upholds voluntary community and opposes involuntary collectivism.

25. _____ perceives the need for prudent restraints upon power and upon human passion.

26. _____ understands that permanence and change must be recognized and reconciled in a vigorous society.

27. _____ believes politics is the art of the possible.

Part V: Historical Conservatism
[Group Theory]

Which does *not* belong in its group?

28. Conservative thinkers:
    a. Edmund Burke
    b. T. S. Eliot
    c. Russell Kirk
    d. Admiral James T. Kirk (Ret.)

29. Conservative leaders:
    a. Ronald Reagan
    b. Theodore Roosevelt
    c. Barry Goldwater
    d. Auric Goldfinger

30. Conservative celebrities:
   a. [Name withheld to protect their career]
   b. [Name withheld to protect their career]
   c. [Name withheld to protect their career]
   d. Sean Penn

Test 2: The Cultural Quiz

It permeates the public's consciousness, and the "mainstream" media obsessively promote the perception to our detriment. Yet polite conservatives won't discuss it. Though it's painful to admit, we must confront the truth: conservatives have a "hip gap." So without further ado, let's discern whether you are culturally attuned to the times:

Part I: The "Mainstream" Media
[Group Theory]

Which does *not* belong in its group?

1. The "mainstream" media deride conservatives as:
    a. Mean
    b. Stupid
    c. Mean and stupid
    d. Cuddly

2. The "mainstream" media's favorite "evil conservatives" are:
   a. Dick Cheney
   b. Joe the Plumber
   c. Darth Vader
   d. Meghan McCain

3. The "mainstream" media oppose conservatives who adopt this policy:
   a. Tax relief
   b. Limited government
   c. Peace through strength
   d. Surrender

4. The "mainstream" media are:
   a. Liberal
   b. Somewhat liberal
   c. Very liberal
   d. Fair

Part II: Pop Culture
[True or False]

Answer the following questions regarding media figures past and present:

5. Snooki is played with cues. *True / False*

6. *The Odd Couple*'s Oscar Madison and Felix Unger were married. *True / False*

7. Jethro Tull starred on *The Beverly Hillbillies*. *True / False*

8. Goldman Sachs was a 1970s "glam rocker." *True / False*

9. The baby on the Gerber label is named Lady Gaga. *True / False*

10. *The Family Guy* airs on the Christian Broadcasting Network. *True / False*

11. Senator John Blutarsky is a RINO. *True / False*

Part III: Modern Life
[Multiple Choice]

To the following queries about modern "lifestyles," the best answer is:

12. In the modern vernacular, a spasm of rage is termed:
    a. "Going postal"
    b. "Losing it"
    c. "Blowing out your diaper"
    d. "Pulling a Howard Dean"

13. "Tweeting" is:
    a. Enticing
    b. Addictive
    c. Sinful
    d. Cured by penicillin

14. "Hip-Hop" is:
    a. A children's game
    b. A one-legged kangaroo
    c. A degenerative ailment requiring replacement surgery
    d. Atonal

15. "Getting baked" most often happens to:
    a. Cookies
    b. Biscuits
    c. Bread
    d. Liberal bloggers in their parents' basements

Answers

What's that you say? "Where are the answers?"
If you have to ask, you've failed.
But here you go.

Philosophical Conservatism Quiz

1–4: (a). 5–10: (True). 11–16: (True—but conservatives know the tenets themselves are false). 17–27: (A conservative). 28: (None of the above). (Trick question, but conservatives know life isn't fair.) 29: (d). 30: (d).

Cultural Quiz

1–4: (d). 5–11: (False). 12–15: (All of the above).

Grades

Pass = Conservative
Fail = Menshevik

(Did I mention the course is pass/fail?)

Keep the Faith

Okay, I was just kidding: you can't fail the test. Conservatism embraces independent thinkers. The point of the exercise was to show how "checklist" conservatism is, in fact, a manifestation of how ideology has infected and hampered the movement.

Remember, unlike New Left loons and "checklist conservatives" who bitch about everything that doesn't fit their myopic ideological platforms, conservatives are philosophical. They believe in reconciling American civilization's enduring pillars of order, justice, and freedom; conserving our inherited and cherished way of life; and preserving America as our blessed sanctuary of liberty.

Abiding Ronald Reagan's observation that "all great change in America begins at the dinner table," conservatives love real life, ordered liberty, and the pursuit of happiness (with no guarantees of finding it). They are aware of their mortality and time's march, so they've got no time for BS (brooding solipsists). Creative, entrepreneurial, patriotic, and admittedly imperfect, conservatives accept their lot and thank the Lord for it.

Dude: conservatives are kick-ass. And we know that the only political "litmus test" that matters is Reagan's measurement of honor: "Let us be sure that those who come after will say of us . . . that in our time we did everything that could be done. We finished the race; we kept them free; we kept the faith."

Friends, for the sake of our nation, we will finish the race and keep the faith.

Class dismissed.

ACKNOWLEDGMENTS

I THANK, THEREFORE I AM

I extend my heartfelt thanks and eternal love to Rita and our children, George, Timothy, and Emilia, for suffering me as I wrote this book in the garage.

I thank my mother, Joan; my late father, Dennis; and my aunt Rosemary for sending me to Catholic Central High School instead of reform school. And I thank my brother, Dennis "Dinky" McCotter; his wife, Shellie; and their kids, Morgan and Abigail, for not yet putting up one of my opponents' yard signs.

I thank all my supporters, be they in the district or following from afar on Twitter, Facebook, or YouTube, and all the sovereign citizens of Michigan's Eleventh Congressional District for electing (or enduring) me as their United States representative.

I thank the U.S. House Republican Caucus for their ideations and fellowship, and I thank some good-hearted Democrats, too, like Collin Peterson (though I will protect their anonymity).

I thank Ed "Horst" McFadden and Jed Donahue for their invaluable suggestions, edits, and most of their comments regarding this book; and Robert Lively, Eric Ueland, Mark "Bulldog" Corallo, "Good Sir" Eric Dezenhall, Mitch "Paisley" Bainwol, Scott "Sports Nation" Rasmussen, and "The Rocker" Christian Josi for all the pearls of wisdom they've thrown at this swine.

I thank the *Red Eye* lads—Greg "Flying Lemur" Gutfeld, Andy Levy, Bill Schulz, and (former producer) Joshua McCarroll—and their guests, who air the best show and "leg chair" on TV.

I thank the entire creative conservative community for their inspiration, however wasted upon me it may be: Robert Davi, Andrew Breitbart, Jon David, Tom and Mary Belle Snow, Mark Burman, Matthew Duda, Mark Pruner, Philippe Martinez (now of Livonia, Michigan), Mike and Maura Flynn, Steve Bannon and David Bossie, Lisa De Pasquale, David Horowitz, Gary Sinise, Karri Turner, Dennis Miller, Adam Baldwin, and all the Hollywood conservatives in that mythic organization whose initials shall remain a tightly held state secret.

I thank John Batchelor, Lee Mason, S. E. Cupp, and Joe Guttilla for the Diet Mountain Dew and sympathy they've served up in the Big Apple.

I thank Dr. Lee Edwards, and the late Dr. Russell Kirk and his vivacious spouse, Annette, for handing down the tablets.

I thank Ramon Palacios, Maria Torres, the Custom Shop, and everyone at the Fender company for making such kick-ass axes.

Finally, for the sake of my immortal soul (and maybe to shave a few seconds off what promises, at best, to be a long stint in purgatory), I thank my namesake, St. Jude, the patron of lost causes like me.

Did I thank the Screaming Lemurs?

INDEX

abortion, legalization of, 146–49
activism, call to, 167
Adams, Abigail, 26, 169–70
Adams, John, 29
Afghanistan, freedom in, 99–102
    See also War for Freedom
AIG (American International
    Group), 66
al-Qaeda, stopping, 93–94
    See also War for Freedom
Alinsky, Saul, 155–57, 160
American Cause, The (Kirk), 18
American citizens. *See also* citizens' rights; human rights
    current challenges of, 19–21
    defending freedom of, 22–26,
        165–71
    individuality of, 62–63, 70–71,
        159
    mental agility of, 18–19, 169–70
    sovereignty of, 23, 25, 152
American influence, 24
American International Group
    (AIG), 66

American Revolution, 31–32
American society
    cultural erosion of, 64–66, 73
    dependency in, 25, 64–67,
        87–88
    globalization and, 62–64
    moral relativism in, 140–44
    revitalization of, 53–57, 74–75,
        164
    salvation of, 165–71
Aristotle, 142
Athenian civilization, the fall of
    ancient, 18

banking industry, 60–61, 66
Belloc, Hilaire, 64–65
biblical references
    1 Chronicles 29:15, 48–49
    Daniel 12:3, 164
    Psalms 90:9, 49
big government. *See also* left-wing
    politics; socialist agenda
    harmful effects of, 69–70,
        72–73

big government *(continued)*
"Servile State" form of, 64–67
"too big to fail" ideology of,
52–53, 60–62, 66, 75
value of limited vs., 20, 23–24,
25
wealth redistribution by, 75–76
Bobbitt, Philip, 51
border security, 83–84
Brooke, Rupert, 170–71
Brothers Karamazov, The (Dostoevsky), 35
Brownson, Orestes, 56–57
budgeting, federal, 76–77
See also economic revitalization
Burke, Edmund
conservative philosophy of,
31–34
on the family unit, 149
on freedom, 169
on hope for reinvigoration,
53–54
business/labor relations, 85–86

Carlson, Allan C., 65
centrism, 69–70, 73
Chesterton, G. K., 65–66, 143
children. *See also* family unit,
weakening of
parental rights concerning,
149–54
safety of unborn, 146–49
China. *See* People's Republic of
China (PRC)
"China Fantasy lobby," 115–17,
129–30, 137
China Human Rights Defenders,
129
Chou En-lai, 31
Christianity, PRC restriction of,
116

1 Chronicles 29:15, 48–49
Churchill, Winston, 105–6
citizens, American. *See* American
citizens
citizens' rights. *See also* human
rights
intellectual property, 82
international laws and, 79
of parents, 149–54
pursuit of happiness, 36–37
real property ownership, 77–78
civil religion, Left's establishment
of a, 40, 42
climate change, 107–8
Clinton, Bill, 120, 128, 149–50
collectivism
industrialization and, 62–63
New Left's agenda of, 20, 23,
39–42
Communist regime of PRC,
115–16, 127, 129, 131
"community disorganization"
agenda, 155–59
Community of Democracies, 135
concurrent receipt, ending,
112–13
conservation policies, 86
conservatism
contrasted with ideology, 21–22
cosmopolitan, 50–53
distinctiveness of nations and,
162
philosophical roots of, 31–34
tenets of, 34–37
CRC (United Nations Convention
on the Rights of the Child),
149–54
"creative destruction," 44, 47–48
Cube and the Cathedral, The
(Weigel), 160
curiosity, power of, 33
cyber warfare, PRC, 123–27

Daniel 12:3, 164
Dawson, Christopher, 143–44, 161
debt, foreign, 120, 134
decentralization through globalization, 63–64, 70–71
defense. *See* national defense
demagogy, dangers of, 17–19
democracy
  Communism vs., 115–16, 129, 131, 137
  inspiring, 24, 165
  international relations and, 132–33
  promotion of, 134–36
"democratic capitalism," 44–48
Democratic Party
  ideology of, 37–39
  New Left takeover of, 39
Demosthenes, 18
dependency, 25, 64–67, 87–88
Destutt de Tracy, Antoine Louis Claude, 29
deterministic materialism, 47–48
dictatorships, 42
diplomacy, international, 132–33
Dostoevsky, Fyodor, 35

economic freedom
  decentralization and, 70–71
  preservation of, 88–91
  subsidiarity for, 87–88
  through financial security, 25, 61
  U.S. foreign debt and, 120, 134
economic revitalization
  financial services industry and, 60–61, 66
  privatization and entrepreneurialism for, 72, 74–75, 82
  tax-and-spend policies and, 67–68, 72, 75–77

education, 82–83, 150–51
Eliot, T. S., 29, 37
"end of history" ideology, 44–48
energy policies, 81
England, decline of, 65
environmentalism, 86, 107–8
espionage, PRC, 123–27
European cultural depravity, 160–61

faith, moral relativism and, 141–44
family unit, weakening of
  legalized abortion, 146–49
  loss of parental authority, 149–54
  through premarital relationships, 144–46
Farris, Michael P., 151, 152–54
fascism, infidel, 93–96
  See also War for Freedom
federal spending, 67–68, 72, 75–77
  See also economic freedom; economic revitalization
Federally Qualified Health Clinics (FQHC), 80
financial security, national, 25, 61
  See also economic freedom
financial services industry, 60–61, 66
First Letter on a Regicide Peace (Burke), 53–54, 167
free trade. *See* trade relations
freedom. *See also* citizens' rights; economic freedom; human rights; War for Freedom
  challenges in preserving, 19–21
  connection between life and, 143–44
  defending, 22–26, 165–71
  inspiring nations to, 24, 165

freedom *(continued)*
    materialism vs., 88–91
    preserving community for,
        157–59
    religious, 116
Freedom Paradigm, 23, 26, 64
freedom trade, 84–85
    See also trade relations
French Revolution, 29–32
Fukuyama, Francis, 44–48

global warming, 107–8
globalism, 50–53
    See also socialist agenda
globalization
    challenges of, 19–21, 168
    decentralization through,
        63–64, 70–71
    "global community" agenda
        and, 160–64
    international laws and, 79
God. *See also* religion
    morality and existence of, 35,
        141–44, 161
    as source of inalienable rights,
        24–25
    as source of power and liberty,
        33, 168
government, limited, 20, 23–25,
    33, 35–36
    See also big government
Gramsci, Antonio, 140, 163
Gramsci's Marxism (Boggs), 140,
    163
Greatest Generation, 19
Greek civilization, the fall of
    ancient, 18
Greenberg, Maurice R., 66
Gutfeld, Greg, foreword by, 11–14

happiness, pursuit of, 36–37
health-care reform, 79–81, 112

hippie movement, 37–40
homeland security, public mis-
    conception of, 106–9
Horowitz, David, 108, 113
housing bubble, 61
How Democracies Perish (Revel),
    25
Hughes, Stuart, 43
human rights. *See also* citizens'
    rights
    erosion of, 77–79
    inalienable, 24–25, 35
    PRC's violations of, 116–17,
        121, 129, 133
    of unborn children, 146–49
Humane Economy, A (Röpke), 61
Hunter, Duncan, 123

ideology. *See also* moral relativ-
    ism
    contrasted with conservatism,
        21–22
    dangers of, 17–19
    "end of history," 44–48
    historical revolutions and,
        29–32
    "New Market State," 51–53
    the pursuit of happiness and,
        36–37
immigration reform, 83–84
inalienable rights, 24–25, 35
income-tax reform, 75–76
individuality, 62–63, 70–71, 159,
    162
industrial welfare state, 62–64
innovation, promotion of, 82,
    87–88
intellectual-property rights, 82
international laws, 79, 149–54
international relations, 94–95,
    105, 132–33
    See also trade relations

Iran, 94–95, 103–4
Iraq, strategy in, 99–102
    See also War for Freedom
Israel, relations with, 105

Jackson, Andrew, 60
Janda, David, 79
John Paul II, Pope, 139, 143,
    148–49
journalism, selective, 106–9

Kennedy, Robert F., 69, 70–71,
    88–89
Kirk, Russell
    on conservatives and ideology,
        43, 48
    on discontent and radicalism,
        18, 30
    on moral imagination, 143
    on moral principles, 54, 164
    on renewal of nations, 60,
        167–68
    on societal change, 12, 169
    on soulless materialism, 71, 170

labor relations, 85–86
labor unions, 85–86
Laogai, PRC's, 116
laws, international, 79, 149–54
left-wing politics. *See also* social-
    ist agenda
    "China Fantasy lobby" of,
        115–17, 129–30, 137
    collectivist agenda of, 20, 23,
        39–42
    cosmopolitan conservatives
        and, 50–53
    cultural assault of, 39–42
    economic theories of, 67–68
    environmentalism and, 107–8
    ideology of, 36–37
legal system reform, 81

Liberty Alliance, 135–36
life
    freedom and, 143–44, 170
    unborn's right to, 146–49
    limited government, 20, 23–25,
        33, 35–36
    See also big government
Lincoln, Abraham, 19, 55–56, 165
Liu Mingfu, 117–18
love
    ending romantic, 144–46
    as object of life, 170
Lucifer, radical alignment with, 155

marriages, weakening of, 144–46
    See also family unit, weakening of
materialism
    deterministic, 47–48
    global, 52
    patriotism over, 88–91
    soulless, 71
McCotter, Thaddeus
    commentary on, 11–14
    vignette on father of, 37–39
military, United States. *See* na-
    tional defense
moral relativism. *See also* social-
    ist agenda
    dangerous effects of, 25–26, 35
    effects on religious faith of,
        141–44
    European cultural depravity
        and, 160–61
    vs. truth, 139–43
morality
    existence of God and, 35,
        141–44, 161
    moral relativism vs., 139–43
    of the War for Freedom, 98–99
Mother Teresa, 147
multiculturalism, promotion of,
    39–42

Nannies in Blue Berets (Farris), 151
national defense. *See also* War for
  Freedom
  border security, 83–84
  Left's agenda of a weak, 42
  necessity of a strong, 131–33
  proper role of, 25
"national disorganization"
  agenda, 160–64
national financial security, 25, 61
  See also economic freedom
NATO (North Atlantic Treaty
  Organization), 132
New Left. *See* left-wing politics
"New Market State" ideology,
  51–53
Nicomachean Ethics (Aristotle),
  142
9/11 attacks, 93–94
Nisbet, Robert, 87, 149, 157–59
North Atlantic Treaty Organiza-
  tion (NATO), 132
*Notes toward the Definition of
  Culture* (Eliot), 37
nuclear containment, 103–4, 132
  See also national defense

Obama administration, 67–68

parental rights, 149–54
patent laws, 82
patriotism over materialism,
  88–91
Pearce, Joseph, 154
People's Liberation Army of
  China (PLA), 117–18, 123–26
People's Republic of China (PRC)
  Communist regime of, 115–16,
    127, 129, 131
  cyber warfare by, 123–27
  dangers of appeasement of, 119,
    128–33, 137

human rights abuses by,
  116–17, 129–30, 133
Iranian relations with, 103–4
political strategies of, 118–23
trade with, 119–20, 128–29, 133
Petraeus, General David, 101–2
philosophy, conservative, 31–34
PLA (People's Liberation Army of
  China), 117–18, 123–26
PRC. *See* People's Republic of
  China (PRC)
principles in defending freedom,
  24–26
pro-choice arguments, refutation
  of, 148
property rights, citizens,' 77–78,
  82
prosperity. *See also* economic
  revitalization
  management/labor solidarity
    for, 85–86
  sources of, 67–68
  wealth redistribution policies
    and, 75–76
  without liberty in PRC,
    119–20, 130
Psalms 90:9, 49
public perception of homeland
  security, 106–9
public vs. private sectors, 67–68

Quest for Community, The (Nisbet), 149

Reagan, Ronald, 72, 85–86, 90,
  103, 166
Red Eye (TV show), 11–12
regulatory reform, 76–77
Reich, Wilhelm, 163
relativism, moral. *See* moral
  relativism
religion. *See also* God

establishment of a civil, 40, 42
moral relativism and, 35,
141–44, 161
restriction of by PRC, 116
Republican Party
2010 elections and, 49–50
failures of, 43–49
Revel, Jean-François, 25
Rice, Condoleezza, 116–17
rights. *See* citizens' rights; human
rights
Roe v. Wade, detrimental effects
of, 146–49
Roosevelt, Franklin D., 98, 109–10
Roosevelt, Theodore, 66, 85, 142,
165
Röpke, Wilhelm, 61, 64, 71
Rousseau, Jean-Jacques, 29,
31–34, 152
*Rules for Radicals: A Pragmatic
Primer for Realistic Radicals*
(Alinsky), 155–57, 160
Russian/Iranian relations, 103–4

Satan, radical alignment with,
155
Schall, Father James V., 142
Schurmann, Franz, 140–41
scriptural references. *See* biblical
references
Second Amendment rights,
79–80
See also citizens' rights
security, border, 83–84
security, national financial, 25, 61
See also economic freedom
self-actualization, 144–46
September 11 attacks, 93–94
"Servile State" of dependency, 25,
64–67, 87–88
sexual relationships, premarital,
144–46

Shanghai Cooperation Organization (SCO), 103–4, 122–23
Sharansky, Natan, 121
Shield of Achilles, The (Bobbitt), 51
*Small Is Still Beautiful: Econom-
ics as If Families Mattered*
(Pearce), 154
socialist agenda. *See also* left-
wing politics
of attacking religious faith,
141–44
"China Fantasy lobby," 115–17,
129–30, 137
of "community disorganization," 155–59
of health-care reform, 79–81,
112
of moral relativism, 139–43
of "national disorganization,"
160–64
of usurping parental authority,
150–51
weakening of the family by,
144–46, 149
of wealth redistribution, 75–76
society, American. *See* American
society
Solzhenitsyn, Aleksandr, 161
sovereignty of American citizens,
23, 25, 152
spending, government, 76–77
See also economic revitalization
subjectivism, moral. *See* moral
relativism
subsidiarity, promotion of, 87–88
Syrian partnership with Iran,
94–95

tax-and-spend policies, 67–68,
72, 75–77
tax credits for employers of veterans, 112

tax reform, income, 75–76
terrorism, defending against,
    93–96
    See also War for Freedom
Third Ways (Carlson), 65
Tkachik, John, 115
"too big to fail" ideology, 52–53,
    60–62, 66, 75
    See also big government
tort reform, 81
totalitarianism, 25
trade relations
    freedom trade, 84–85
    materialism of, 47–48
    with PRC, 119–20, 128–29, 133
truth, moral relativism vs.,
    139–43

Unholy Alliance (Horowitz), 108
unions, labor, 85–86
United Nations, 103–4, 134–35
United Nations Convention on
    the Rights of the Child (CRC),
    149–54

Van Bueren, Geraldine, 150–52
veterans services, 111–13

War for Freedom. *See also* na-
    tional defense
    endurance in, 105–6, 109–10
    Israeli relations and, 105
    moral principles of, 93–97
    nuclear containment and,
        103–4
    public perception of, 106–9
    strategy in, 99–102
war protestors, 38–39
wealth redistribution policies,
    75–76
Weigel, George, 160
Willetts, David, 162
women, harm of abortions to, 148
Wordsworth, William, 90, 168

Xia, Renée, 129

Zhou Xiaochuan, 121–22